LAMBORGHINI COUNTACH

Paul Clark

CONTENTS

Foulis

Haynes

ISBN 0 85429 553 4

A FOULIS Motoring Book

First published 1986

© Haynes Publishing Group

Published by:

Haynes Publishing Group,
Sparkford, Near Yeovil,
Somerset BA22 7JJ

Haynes Publications Inc.
861 Lawrence Drive, Newbury
Park, California 91320, USA

**British Library Cataloguing in
Publication Data**

Clark, Paul
 Lamborghini Countach Super profile.–
 (Super profile)
 1. Countach automobile–History
 I. Title   II. Series
 629.2'222   TL215.L6/
 ISBN 0-85429-553-4

Editor: Mansur Darlington
Dust jacket design: Rowland
Smith
Series photographer: Andrew
Morland
Road tests: Courtesy of *Autocar,
Motor* and *Thoroughbred &
Classic Cars*
Page layout: Chris Hull
Printed in England, by:
J.H. Haynes & Co. Ltd

Further titles in this series will be published at regular
intervals. For information on new titles please contact
your bookseller or write to the publisher.

FOREWORD

Born out of a company founded only 22 years ago, the Lamborghini Countach (pronounced 'Coon-tash' incidentally) is perhaps the pinnacle of supercar thinking, with a combination of styling, engineering, technology and performance that today sets it apart from other cars in the same category. It is without doubt the greatest, the most outrageous of supercars; a blatant expression of power, speed and sheer eccentricity that today has no equal.

By all accounts, Ferruccio Lamborghini is a remarkable man. Having made his fortune producing tractors in the years immediately following the Second World War, he was able to indulge himself in one of his great passions, fast cars, and by 1960 had owned quite a range of exotic machinery. It was his dissatisfaction with most of them that inspired him to set up his own company to manufacture what was in his mind the ultimate supercar, one that would fulfil all his requirements, the perfect car.

It is not hard to imagine the difficulties that might be encountered in setting up a project like this: indeed, to many it would probably be merely a pipe dream. Yet to Lamborghini it was almost a necessity. His determination and sheer will to succeed are an example to everyone.

How many people thought the Lamborghini concern was just a flash in the pan when the first car was exhibited at Turin in 1963 is open to speculation, but Ferruccio Lamborghini had the determination to see the project through. Economic problems, high taxation on exotic cars and the OPEC energy crisis of the early Seventies have all befallen the factory but it has weathered these storms, and more, admirably.

In the preparation of this book, many people have helped and to them I should like to record my most grateful thanks.

Finding cars to photograph and examine would have been a daunting task had it not been for assistance from the Lamborghini Owners Club secretary, Barry Martina, and dedicated enthusiasts like Barry Robinson whose lovely LP500S is depicted within these pages. Also, my thanks to Andrew Morland for photographing the cars and providing some of the pictures.

In a sense it has been a difficult task producing this *Super Profile*. In 22 years, the name of Lamborghini has become associated with the very highest standards in fast motoring and although the Countach has been in production for over a decade already, the story is far from finished. The past ten years of Lamborghini history have seen more changes than many manufacturers are likely to see in twice the time but despite this the name lives on. Currently nearly 950 Countaches have been built, a remarkable achievement for this type of car, and production looks assured for the future. At present, the factory produces some 13 cars per month which, at the time of writing, each retail at £68,530. Even though back in 1974, Ferruccio Lamborghini sold his interests in the company he founded in 1963, his name still appears on some of the most renowned and successful GT cars in the world. He is a remarkable man, as remarkable as his cars in many ways and to him motoring enthusiasts from all over the world owe a debt of gratitude.

Paul Clark

HISTORY

Ferruccio Lamborghini was born on April 28, 1916, in the small Italian farming village of Renazzo di Cento, Ferrara. From an early age he showed a keen aptitude for anything mechanical and was far more attracted to a life of engineering than one of farming. Leaving the community after a short time, he headed for Bologna where he obtained a degree in industrial engineering. The outbreak of the Second World War shortly after that saw him drafted into the Italian services on the island of Rhodes where, owing to his strong powers of ingenuity, he was set to work on vehicle maintenance in an area affected more than most by the problems of poor supply. Even when the island was captured by the allies his talents were realised and he was set to work on the repair of their vehicles.

When at last hostilities ceased, Lamborghini turned his attention to producing tractors to help raise his country to its feet after suffering the devastation of war years. Initially his work involved the building of tractors from spare parts and materials he could obtain from the numerous abandoned army camps and surplus stations and his first tractor, so built, emerged in 1947.

By 1949, however, his supplies were dwindling and he was forced to look elsewhere. A government grant allowed Lamborghini to set up a proper manufacturing facility, *Trattori Lamborghini SpA,* and by 1960 he had become one of the country's leading tractor makers. Further industrial dabbling resulted in the founding of a company manufacturing heating and air-conditioning equipment, *Lamborghini Bruciatori,* and these two ventures were sufficient to turn him into a wealthy industrialist. Reflecting his success, he was able to indulge himself in one of his great passions, exotic motor cars, and owned a range of fast cars including some of the products of the Ferrari factory at Modena.

But he was disappointed with the cars, though his driving techniques always attracted diverse comment from Ferrari himself. He said Lamborghini had no idea of how to drive Ferraris, equating them in some way to the tractors for which he was so renowned.

It is thought this exchange is what finally turned Lamborghini to the idea of producing his own high performance car, one which, in his mind, would fulfill all his requirements and upstage the opposition at the same time.

It is not difficult to imagine the problems that might be involved with setting up a factory to produce cars of the type Lamborghini had in mind. Fifties Italy had seen an economic boom and Lamborghini had profited from his heating and tractor making concerns so much so that he had amassed a considerable fortune in a relatively short time. In the early Sixties he put his mind to the idea of producing his perfect car and set about finding the right people to come up with the designs needed.

At the heart of his design team was Gian Paolo Dallara, a brilliant engineer who had worked for Ferrari after graduating from the Technical Institute of Milan in 1960. In 1961 he moved to Maserati where he worked under his cousin, Giulio Alfieri, who was responsible for the company's racing department. Dallara was only 24 when Lamborghini approached him in 1963. Giotto Bizzarrini had had experience both of Alfa Romeo and Ferrari where he was largely responsible for the production of the fabled GTO. Leaving Ferrari in 1961, he went to work on a freelance basis and completed several designs for the Iso Rivolta chassis which was by then nearing completion. Lamborghini's interest in Bizzarrini stemmed from the fact that he had on his files designs for a 12-cylinder engine of 1.5-litres, originally intended for Formula 1 racing. With its V-formation and four overhead camshafts, this was what Lamborghini wanted for his proposed car, and though the basic idea was accepted, he commissioned from Bizzarrini designs for an engine of 3.5 litres.

The third member of Lamborghini's trio of engineers was New Zealand-born Bob Wallace. Wallace had worked as a works department driver for both Maserati and Ferrari and was working with the *Scuderia Serenissima* when Lamborghini made his acquaintance. Although he had received a good offer to return to Ferrari as a test driver, Wallace decided against it and took up Lamborghini's offer to work for him on his new project. To assist Dallara in the design department, Lamborghini hired Paolo Stanzani, at that time aged only 25, a graduate engineer of the University of Bologna.

Initially, work on the new car took place in the special developments area of Lamborghini's tractor factory at Cento, but meanwhile a brand new and ultra-modern plant was being built specifically for the car project at Sant' Agata Bolognese, some 20km from Modena. Lamborghini reasoned that if the car project failed, he could use the new factory to increase his tractor output.

By July 1963, Bizzarrini's design for the new V12 engine had been turned into a production reality and the engine ran for the first time on a dynamometer. It produced 360bhp at 8000rpm (SAE) using six vertical choke Weber carburettors. Originally, the engine had been designed by Bizzarrini to produce 400bhp at 11,000rpm but Lamborghini was not receptive to the idea of using the engine in competition. Clearly this was what the design team had had in mind from the outset but Lamborghini was adamant his cars were for road use only. He was sure that he should not tackle two problems at once; his thoughts for the moment were concentrated into producing his ultimate GT car – even though he did not dislike motorsport, this was the course of action that would be taken. Bizzarrini, however, did not agree with his thinking and refused Lamborghini's decision to build a more docile road-tuned engine based on the same design, and consequently walked out.

Ironically, it was the Modenese workshop of Neri e Bonacini, for whom Bizzarrini had originally worked, that was producing the chassis which would carry the new engine. It featured a tube frame and all-independent suspension with coil springs. Unlike any Ferrari of the day it was offered with a ZF five-speed gearbox.

The job of the body design had been entrusted to the *Carrozzeria* Franco Scaglione. Lamborghini was extremely concerned about the appearance of the new car and insisted Scaglione incorporated many of the design features of current cars that he liked, including ideas from Jaguar and Aston Martin. Scaglione had worked for Bertone for eight years and was partially responsible for such creations as the Alfa Romeo Sprint Speciale,

with its characteristic rounded lines. Indeed this was the hallmark of his designs and the finished drawings for Lamborghini's new car had a mixture of angles and curves that was looked upon as slightly fussy by the critics of the day; nevertheless it was built by Sargiotto of Turin and fitted to the prototype chassis just in time for the 1963 Turin Motor Show, held in October. Perhaps not unexpectedly, praise for the magnificent V12 was great, but the body styling brought considerable criticism and caused Lamborghini quickly to entrust a new design to *Carrozzeria* Touring, the same company which produced the very beautiful Aston Martin bodies of the day built on the patented *Superleggera* principle.

With changes simplifying the engine including a wet sump and less expensive carburettors, the new car, the 350GT, went on display at the 1964 Geneva Motor Show. The chassis had been refined by Dallara and was now rated among the very best in the world. Contemporary road tests hailed the new Lamborghini as a significant landmark in the history of the GT car.

There followed, in 1964, a blow to the company that can only be described as unfortunate: the Italian government placed a heavy purchase tax on the sale of exotic cars which heavily depressed the market and caused considerable gloom.

Thankfully, the company's finances were such that it was able to weather the storm and Lamborghini set his mind to producing a series of new models for the 1965 Turin Motor Show.

Among the new exhibits at this show was a chassis designated TP400 which carried a transverse rendering of the V12 engine in 4.0-litre form, ahead of the rear wheels. At the same time, *Carrozzeria* Touring had gone bankrupt forcing Lamborghini to turn to Bertone for a design with

which to clothe the chassis. The whole thing was the brainchild of Stanzani, Dallara and Wallace who had conceived the idea in their own time and then presented the complete package to Lamborghini who excitedly gave the go-ahead for its completion. Of course, this model was the basis for the Miura which marked a turning point in the history of Lamborghini. By this time, Lamborghini-designed and built gearboxes and differentials had been put into production doing away with the ZF and Salisbury units previously employed. The cars were now, as Lamborghini had always wanted, virtually in-house productions.

The Miura was an instant success and survived from 1966 to early 1973. In all, about 760 were made of all types, the final version, the P400SV, being radically different in terms of performance from the first P400 though still retaining the beautiful clean lines of the original.

In fact the Miura was the subject of continual improvement. By the late Sixties, the 400GT, a derivation of the original 350GTV, was getting somewhat long in the tooth and Lamborghini commissioned *Carrozzeria* Marrazzi to design a new car. The result was the Islero, a very conservative-looking creation that was in fact extremely fast, being almost a match for the renowned Miura performance. The Islero made its début at the 1968 Geneva Motor Show alongside the four-seater Espada, a remarkable amalgam of practicality and performance. The Espada was derived from Lamborghini's 1967 show car, the Marzal, which was a futuristic design study with a V6 2.0-litre 175bhp engine and bodywork styled by Bertone.

With so many exciting cars being produced in the Sixties, enthusiasm at Lamborghini was very high, not least from Ferruccio himself. However towards the end of the decade, his personal interest in the car factory waned somewhat and, regarded by many as a strange move at the time, he promoted Paolo Stanzani to the role of general manager of the factory, much to the disgust of Gian Paolo Dallara. The thought of his assistant assuming the role of chief designer was too much and Dallara left Lamborghini in 1968 to join De Tomaso who had on the stocks at that time a design for a Formula One racing car. The lack of competition involvement with Lamborghini had also frustrated Dallara who had always longed to be involved with a racing project.

Stanzani's promotion coincided with the introduction of a very beautiful but hopelessly impractical Miura Roadster, but by the early Seventies designs for a brand new and very exciting project were already in hand.

Even though production of the Miura, with the P400SV, was now in its final stages, demand was still very strong and indeed the car sold well. Bob Wallace had been experimenting with his own lightweight Miura which had a considerably uprated engine and a reputed top speed of 180mph . . . Clearly he was playing with the prospect of a very fast addition to the Lamborghini range, a radically new car that would perfect the shortcomings experienced with the Miura, which was very fast but which had somewhat unpredictable handling: the front end had a tendency to lighten progressively as speed increased.

In 1970, Lamborghini diversified its range and produced the 2.5-litre V8-engined Urraco P250, mainly to compete with the smaller-engined Ferraris and Porsches. There was also a considerable market in America for a car of this type and the US distributor was confident he could sell at least 200 a year. Although the idea basically was sound, the problems in Lamborghini gearing up to produce a brand new model were immense and production of the car didn't in fact start until 1972.

While the Urraco was being productionised, however, another landmark in Lamborghini's history had passed: the 1971 Geneva Motor Show had witnessed the arrival of another Lamborghini, something that Wallace had dreamed of and the result of Lamborghini's collaboration with Bertone. The first Countach had arrived, the LP500.

The fruit of much hard work, the new car was barely finished before the show; the latest variant of the Miura, the P400SV, was on display but it was the Countach that stole the limelight. The car's design was revolutionary, with its longitudinally mounted 5.0-litre V12 positioned ahead of the rear wheels and with the five-speed gearbox in front of it. An ingenious solution to the problem of getting the drive from the gearbox back to the final drive and the rear wheels had been arrived at by enclosing the output shaft of the gearbox in an all-enveloping housing in the sump: in effect, the driveshaft ran under the crankshaft. This eliminated all the problems associated with long and complicated gear linkages to a rear-mounted gearbox and final drive and enabled the gearshift to be of exceptional quality.

From a styling point of view, the bodywork was stunning, with doors that opened upwards and a long sweeping nose which accentuated the overall 'wedge' shape. The design was pure and purposeful, inspired by Bertone's earlier design exercise, the Alfa Romeo-based Carabo which was penned back in 1968.

The word 'Countach' derives from a Torinese expression of amazement and it is believed to have been uttered by one of the Sant 'Agata workers on seeing the new Lamborghini for the first time. His reaction is understandable as here was a car that was revolutionary in design and concept, whose stunning looks were the culmination of all that Lamborghini had learned.

The prototype LP500 was built in a great hurry in order to meet that 1971 Geneva show deadline. The car's futuristic lines drew admiration in plenty but few thought the car would become a production reality. But then, the Miura had made its debut as a show special – and that car had been in production for six years! True, the Countach was not practical, but, as Wallace often said, Lamborghinis were always meant to be nothing but performance machines, with everything taking second place to speed and handling. The Countach fulfilled those observations admirably. Ironically, though, the new car had a roomier cockpit than the Miura and even had a usable boot located behind the engine, even if it was centrally heated by the car's exhaust system!

To get it built in time for the car's début at Geneva, the chassis was a hurriedly put together sheet metal affair welded over a tubular framework. Nevertheless, Wallace's initial testing of the prototype proved it was really very competent despite the limited amount of serious testing he was able to carry out as both Bertone and Lamborghini wanted the car for promotional purposes. After they had finished, Wallace had it back for a more intensive testing programme, but it took three years to develop the original show Countach into a productionable prospect.

After the sensation of the new car had died down, things got back to normal in 1972: productionising of the Urraco P250 began in earnest on the strength of the American distributor's promise and 200 cars were built. The outcome was that only 38 were sold, leaving Lamborghini with severe cash flow problems. Coupled with that came news that a large Bolivian export order for Lamborghini's tractors had been cancelled owing to political difficulties; 5000 tractors were unsold at the Cento factory. Ferruccio Lamborghini was beginning to have worries about the tractor firm and decided to sell 51 per cent of his interests in the car operation to keep the Cento factory afloat the buyer was Swiss industrialist, Georges-Henri Rossetti.

The Countach testing programme ended in 1974 with the prototype LP500 being crash-tested into a concrete wall at the British Motor Industry Research Association proving ground. Productionising of the car was complete and Lamborghini was obliged to write off the car in this way to obtain the necessary E-marking which would allow him to start building the LP400.

The first LP400 made its début at the 1973 Geneva Motor Show but it wasn't until 1975 that the first 'customer' versions appeared, so shaky were the company's labour relations and finances at the time. Although outwardly similar to the LP500, the LP400 incorporated solutions to many of the problems found in the development car. On the outside, the most obvious changes were the addition of airboxes aft of the doors and NACA air ducts below them to improve airflow to the engine, always a problem on the prototype. The original and troublesome 'periscope' rear view mirror had been dropped in favour of conventional interior and wing-mounted units, and different roadwheels were fitted, shod with

Michelin XWX tyres. Inside, conventional instruments replaced the digital display of the original car and the upholstery made much use of suede although its design remained largely unaltered.

Under the bonnet things were radically different. Trouble had been experienced with the 5.0-litre engine of the prototype and for this reason Stanzani chose to revert to the original and well-tried 4.0-litre V12 unit with its unique and successful 'driveshaft under crankshaft' arrangement. Two six-plug Marelli distributors were adopted for the ignition system in place of the single 12-plug unit fitted to the LP500 and two water radiators were fitted, one on each side of the engine, fed by the NACA ducts and air intakes fitted behind the doors. Oil cooling was achieved by the single oil radiator mounted in the right-hand front wing.

Magnesium 'Elektron' castings were used for many Countach components, including the clutch bellhousing, cam covers and casing for the oil pump but early experience with the wheel hub carriers, which were also of magnesium, had shown they were prone to gradual deterioration and these, therefore, were changed for similar castings of light alloy.

At last the Countach was born. It made a big impression on the supercar market in 1975 and praise from the motoring press was indeed great. The rapturous response was, however, dulled by a sad sequence of events that marked yet another turning point

at Lamborghini. By 1974, Ferruccio Lamborghini had sold the remaining 49 per cent of his holdings in the car company to a friend of Georges-Henri Rossetti, René Leimer, after continued ill health had prevented Rossetti from assuming his responsibilities to the full. After 12 years of remarkable success in producing his dream cars, Lamborghini no longer had any part in the business he founded back in 1963 . . .

Bob Wallace was not happy with Lamborghini's departure and sensed a change in the company's attitude and dedication. Political and economic problems in Italy were taking their toll as well and in the end he, too, decided to leave. The failure of the American order and the problems at Sant' Agata proved too much for Stanzani also and he resigned at the beginning of 1975. René Leimer appointed a new board, with Stanzani's replacement, Gian Paolo Dallara, and a new managing director, Pier Capellini, taken on to improve the situation.

One of Capellini's first tasks was to sack the American distributor in favour of one with more realistic ideas. Demand for the LP400 Countach was encouraging and already a full year's production had been sold. The problem was in getting the cars built.

Another new project was launched in 1975, specifically aimed at the American market when Leimer finally realised there was no real demand for the Urraco in the United States. Instigated by Capellini, this was the Silhouette, of which 52 were built. Despite its 3.0-litre V8 engine and top speed of 162mph, overall production was a great disappointment, and though the Silhouette was an important model in Lamborghini's range, development of the Countach took precedence.

Millionaire enthusiast Walter Wolf had commissioned a very special Countach to be built using the revolutionary new Pirelli P7 tyres which had just been announced. At this time, money was very short at Lamborghini and the company could not finance the extra development required to modify the standard car's suspension to accept the new tyres. In view of this, Wolf paid for the work to be done himself. By doing so, he not only obtained a unique LP400 but also ensured that the company was able to make full use of the potential of these remarkable new tyres.

The first car built specifically to accept them was the new Silhouette, displayed for the first time at the Geneva Motor Show in 1976. The results of this extra development work ultimately benefited the Countach so much so that a revised version, the Countach S, was launched in 1978. Although there were no changes to the engine or power output, the car's chassis came in for a good deal of modification. The front suspension was altered to cater for the different characteristics of the low profile tyres, the original Girling disc brakes were changed in favour of Italian-built ATE units, and the springs and shock absorbers were relocated together with a new anti-roll bar to make the front end stiffer. At the rear, the original reversed A-arms were replaced by twin lower links with a new design of hub carrier supporting the 300mm ventilated discs with four-piston calipers.

Externally the Countach S featured flared wheel arch extensions made in glassfibre, necessary to cover the enormous P7 tyres, 205/50 VR15 on the front, 345/35 VR15 on the rear. There was also a revised front end incorporating a glassfibre spoiler and 'bumper' which blended into the line of the wheel arches. Many of these modifications had stemmed from the special Countaches built specially for Walter Wolf, and in many ways his cars resembled the S models even though they were merely modified

LP400s.

Since he had become involved with Lamborghini, René Leimer had made considerable efforts to diversify Lamborghini's products. Two projects stand out as being of significant importance in the company's history. The first was a deal he tied up with the German manufacturer, BMW, whereby he would take on the development of a new model in the BMW range, codenamed E-26, eventually to become the M1. The engineering would be undertaken by BMW in anticipation of building 400 cars to make the M1 eligible for Group 4 racing. Accordingly, the Italian government provided a large loan for Leimer on the strength of the BMW tie-up, which he used partly to bale out the company and partly to finance another deal to produce an all-terrain vehicle for the American Mobility Technology International organisation. This was the Cheetah, a large four-wheel drive machine with a 360cu in Chrysler V8 engine and a top speed of 104mph. This machine was sent to the States where unfortunately, it was destroyed in testing after having used most of the government loan in its development. As the BMW M1 was due to start production in July 1977, Leimer approached BMW for further financial assistance but was refused, and the lack of funds eventually brought production of the Urraco and Silhouette to a halt.

Lamborghini was now in a desperate situation. It was rumoured that Walter Wolf was interested in buying the company early in 1978 but Leimer's partner Rosetti was not keen on the deal and would not allow it. As a last resort, Leimer turned to the Italian government for a two year period of controlled administration (an arrangement provided for within the Italian bankruptcy laws), a request which was accepted.

Consequently the court ordered

all debts to be suspended for a period of two years, and appointed an adminstrator, Alessandro Artesi, to the company to work in conjunction with Ubaldo Sgarzi, Lamborghini's sales manager for the past 12 years. Although production of the Urraco and Silhouette was still uncertain at the time, orders had been coming in steadily for the new Countach S and nearly 50 cars were built by the end of 1978. The Espada ceased production late in the year.

During the time Lamborghini was under controlled adminstration by the Italian Government, the German importer for Lamborghini, ex-BMW racing star, Hubert Hahne, became interested in negotiating a takeover deal. Hahne had built several replicas of Bob Wallace's Miura-based Jota back in the early Seventies and had requested that Lamborghini build a turbocharged version of the V12 for display at the 1979 Geneva Motor Show. This idea went only as far as an amateur mock up which didn't help Lamborghini's credibility at this delicate stage. Nevertheless, negotiations were complete by the end of September 1979 and Hahne assumed the responsibilities of general manager in November.

There followed a series of events which ended in control of the company being handed back to the government early in 1980, owing to some of the agreement conditions not being fulfilled. One of these was that an agreed amount of money should be paid to all creditors in the settlement of debts; when the time came to pay, however, the money was not available and the Germans were finally rejected by the Italian court. At this time between six and eight Countaches were being built per month for which all the suppliers were paid in cash with the money earned from previous sub-contracts.

With renewed faith, Bertone

exhibited at the 1980 Turin Motor Show a new model, the Athon, indicating that he was trying to set the record straight for Lamborghini after years of financial and political problems.

The car, a two-seater convertible, with the 3.5-litre V8 engine based on that of the Urraco, seemed to reassure potential buyers of the company because, during that summer, negotiations began with the Franco-Swiss Mimran Group, whose president, Patrick Mimran, 24, agreed to a plan whereby the company would be leased to them until the controlled administration period ended in May 1981. Mimran officially took over the company on September 1, 1980, renaming it Nuova Autombili Ferruccio Lamborghini SpA.

1981 saw the introduction of the Jalpa, a development of the Silhouette powered by a 3.5-litre V8 engine, and another four-wheel drive vehicle, codenamed LM-001, a successor to the Cheetah fitted with a 353bhp version of the 4.0-litre V12.

As far as the Countach was concerned, the latest version, the LP500S was launched in 1982, fitted with the 5.0-litre version of the V12, actually of 4754cc capacity, developing 375bhp (DIN). This was the ultimate development so far seen, its outrageous rear wing to keep the tail down being reminiscent of an aircraft tailplane and helping to set off its overwhelmingly aggressive appearance.

For 1985, the Countach S *Quattrovalvole* was launched, with a revised engine and four-valve heads, a higher compression ratio (9.5:1 rather than 9.2:1), a larger stroke giving a capacity of 5167cc and a different carburettor arrangement using a set of downdraught 44DCNF Webers in place of the 45DCOE units used previously. All this, of course, meant extra power – much more power. With no less than a claimed 455bhp at 7000rpm and a massive 369lb ft of torque at 5200rpm, performance was astonishing. *Autocar* magazine managed a top speed of 179.2mph with 0-60mph in 4.9 seconds during their 'Autotest' of May 29, 1985, the highest figure ever recorded for any car in the road test series.

"Bearing in mind that no one buys a Countach for normal reasons," wrote *Autocar's* testers in conclusion, "the *Quattrovalvole* Countach is presently the Supercar to beat."

That Lamborghini has managed to weather so many storms is remarkable in its relatively short lifespan. At the time of writing, the company's future seems assured, with some 950 Countaches now built. Even though reference to the Countach being possibly the last of the supercars has been made in the past, surely Ferruccio Lamborghini himself would be proud of the achievement of his initial dream – to build the ultimate supercar? For that is certainly what the Countach is, the ultimate supercar.

EVOLUTION

The Lamborghini Countach has undergone many changes during its fifteen year lifespan, but in all that time the basic shape of the car has remained essentially the same, remarkable testimony to the purity of Bertone's original design. Of the bodywork changes, most of these had been achieved by Spring 1971.

Spring 1971: Original Countach LP500 announced at Geneva Motor Show, powered by 5.0-litre V12 engine.

Spring 1973: First Countach LP400 introduced at the Geneva Motor Show, powered by 4.0-litre version of V12 engine. (LP500 prototype crash-tested to E-mark the car for production.) External differences from prototype included fitment of airscoops behind doors to aid engine cooling, and NACA ducts below windows to improve airflow to radiators. Original periscope rearview mirror dropped in favour of conventional one, different road wheels fitted with Michelin XWX tyres. Inside had conventional instruments rather than digital displays. Twin six-plug Marelli distributors fitted to ignition system in place of original 12-plug unit. Some magnesium castings,

eg wheel hub carriers, changed for conventional light alloy parts owing to experience of deterioration.

Spring 1975: Walter Wolf's first Countach tailor-made, inspiring Lamborghini to include many of this car's changes in production models. Specification included fitment of new Pirelli P7 tyres.

Spring 1978: Countach S introduced. Suspension modifications as follows: location points of springs and shock absorbers altered to decrease variation in movement; new front anti-roll bar fitted. New ball and roller axle bearing employed, together with new hub carriers (see above). Girling brake calipers replaced with ATE units and new steering box fitted. Wheels (front) fitted with 205/50 VR15 Pirelli P7 tyres. Rear suspension changed to two sets of twin parallel links, with larger hub bearing. Larger brake discs, of 284mm, fitted with four piston ATE calipers. Wheels (rear) fitted with 345/35 VR15 Pirelli P7 tyres. Handbrake relocated to right of driver, together with revised actuation. Wheel arches enlarged to accept new tyres, extensions being made of glassfibre, together with front 'spoiler' moulding, also in glassfibre. Rear wing fitted.

Spring 1979: Mock turbocharged V12 displayed at Geneva Motor Show; no further development undertaken.

Autumn 1979: Dashboard enlarged with bigger instruments. Redesigned road wheels with oval holes.

1982: Countach LP500S introduced with 5.0-litre V12, 375bhp.

1985: 'Quattrovalvole' announced with differences as follows: four-valve heads (giving a total of 48 valves), higher compression ratio (9.5:1 rather than 9.2:1), larger stroke giving capacity of 5167cc, Weber 44DCNF downdraught carburettors instead of 45DCOE side-draught set-up. 455bhp at 7000rpm (DIN), 0-60mph in 4.9 seconds, top speed (measured) 179.2mph *(Autocar)*.

SPECIFICATION

Countach LP500

Model	Prototype
Number made	One built in 1971
Drive configuration	Mid-engine; rear wheel drive. Mounted longitudinally ahead of rear wheels.
Engine	Lamborghini 60 degree V12, four overhead camshafts, 4971cc. Compression ratio: 11.5:1 Bore 85mm, stroke 73mm. Maximum power 440bhp (DIN) at 7400rpm; maximum torque 366lb ft (DIN) at 5000rpm. Six sidedraught Weber twin-choke carburettors. Two-valve cylinder heads.
Transmission	Five-speed manual gearbox driving to Lamborghini differential mounted at rear of engine via special under-crank driveshaft. Hydraulic single-plate clutch. Automatic not available.
Chassis	Tubular steel structure with independent suspension on all wheels: parallel wishbone arms, coil springs, telescopic shock absorbers and anti-roll bars. Wheelbase: 96.5in (2.45m). Track: front 59.1in (1.50m), rear 59.8in (1.52m). Overall length 163in (4.14m), width 74.4in (1.89m), height 42.1in (1.07m).
Steering	Rack & pinion. Turning circle 42.7ft.
Brakes	Girling ventilated disc brakes on all four wheels, hydraulically operated via dual circuit system with twin servos.

Wheels and tyres	Magnesium alloy wheels (front) 7$\frac{1}{2}$J x 14in, (rear) 9$\frac{1}{2}$J x 14in. Tyres, front 205/70 VR 14, rear 215/70 VR 14.
Body design	Bertone two-seater, horizontally hinged doors.
Performance	Top speed 186mph (est) No other figures available

Countach LP400

Period current	1973 – 1978
Number made	150
Drive configuration	Mid-engine, rear wheel drive. All alloy.
Engine	Lamborghini 60 degree V12 mounted longitudinally ahead of rear wheels, four overhead camshafts, 3929cc. Compression ratio: 10.5:1. Bore 82mm, stroke 62mm. Maximum power 375bhp (DIN) at 8000rpm; maximum torque 266lb ft (DIN) at 5000rpm. Six sidedraught 45DCOE 23 Weber twin-choke carburettors. Two-valve cylinder heads.
Transmission	Five-speed gearbox driving to ZF limited-slip differential mounted at rear of engine, via special under-crank driveshaft. Hydraulic single-plate Fichtel & Sachs clutch. Automatic not available.

Gear ratios:

1st	9/24:1
2nd	7.24:1
3rd	5.36:1
4th	4.05:1
5th	3.19:1
Final drive	4.09:1

Chassis	Tubular steel chassis with aluminium panels. Front suspension: unequal length A-arms, coil springs, dampers and anti-roll bar. Rear suspension: upper lateral links, lower reversed A-arms, upper and lower trailing arms, dual coil springs, dual shock absorbers, anti-roll bar. Dimensions as LP500.
Steering	Rack and pinion. Turning circle 42.7ft
Brakes	Girling ventilated disc brakes on all four wheels, hydraulically operated with twin servos.
Wheels and tyres	As LP500
Body design	As LP500
Performance	Top speed: 175mph (est) 0-60mph 5.6sec Standing $\frac{1}{4}$ mile 14.1sec

Countach LP400S

Period Current	1978 – 1982
Number Made	234
Specification as for LP400 except for:	Maximum power: 353bhp at 7500rpm (DIN)
	Maximum torque: 267lb ft at 5500rpm (DIN)
Wheels and tyres	
Front:	Campagnolo cast alloy wheels with 205/50 VR15 Pirelli P7 tyres. Wheel size: 15in x 8$\frac{1}{2}$in.
Rear:	Campagnolo cast alloy wheels with 345/35 VR15 Pirelli P7 tyres. Wheels size: 15in x 12in.

Countach LP500S

Period Current:	1982–1985
Specification as for LP400S except for:	Engine 4754cc. Bore 69mm Stroke 85.5mm.
	Maximum power: 375bhp (DIN) at 7000rpm

Countach 'Quattrovalvole' 5000S

Period current	1985 -*
Engine	Lamborghini 60 degree all alloy V12 mounted longitudinally ahead of rear wheels, four overhead camshafts, 5167cc. Compression ratio: 9.5:1. Bore 85.5mm, stroke 75mm. Maximum power 455bhp (DIN) at 7000rpm, maximum torque 369lb ft (DIN) at 5200rpm. Six downdraught twin-choke Weber 44DCNF carburettors. Four-valve cylinder heads.
Performance	Top speed 179mph
	0-60mph 4.9sec
	Standing $\frac{1}{4}$ mile 13sec

Still in production. Total Countach production as at January 1986: 923 of all types

DRIVING IMPRESSION

Sitting next to the kerb in a side street in one of North London's leafier suburbs, Barry Robinson's brilliant red Lamborghini Countach LP500S has all the poise and aggression of a vehicle built primarily for speed.

Viewed from the front, the car has a peculiar 'praying mantis' stance accentuated by the sweeping lines of its flanks and the enormous aeroplane-style wing sitting aft of the rear wheel arches.

A quick walk around the car rams home the purposeful character of this car with devastating effect; the front spoiler, a mere two or three inches from the tarmac, blends with the front wheel arches which hide the enormous Pirelli P7 tyres. The single windscreen wiper with its pantograph action sweeps the vast windscreen which lies at a crazy angle over the cramped cockpit and its two leather-upholstered seats. On the sides, huge NACA ducts perforate the bodywork and assist the two air intake 'ears' behind the cabin to direct air to the radiators, clearly visible through the side ducting. Even bigger wheel arches hide the still more massive Pirelli P7s – 12 inches wide – from sight and that huge wing adds balance and stability to this arrow of a car, so low that it stands only as high as one's waist.

Four stubby exhaust pipes protruding at the rear give a mere hint of the power and excitement that lies under the simply louvred rear engine cover, but the word 'Lamborghini', written in subtle lower case script, quite small, on the left hand side of the flat rear panel, says it all.

This is the car we had come to drive, a car that looked more suitable for the track than a London street on a cold autumn day.

Opening the horizontally hinged doors is easy as they are assisted by a gas strut which pushes the whole thing almost to 90 degrees. The resultant opening reveals an expanse of upholstered sill some 1^1/2 feet wide and it is on this that you must sit in order to swing your legs into the footwell while the rest of you slides into the bucket of the leather seat.

Now you're inside the car. A quick look around confirms it is small inside, though you are separated from the passenger by the huge transmission tunnel with the gearlever perched on top in its gate. Ahead is the instrument pod and the small thick-rimmed leather steering wheel which is adjustable for rake and height. Altering the seat position is difficult mainly because it has no more than a couple of inches of movement but by juggling with the steering wheel adjustments a satisfactory compromise can be reached. Pull the door down hard and it shuts with a reassuring 'clunk'. There's a buzzer which indicates when the door is open, a useful feature as it's impossible to tell if it's only half on the latch.

The rake of the windscreen is extraordinary; you cannot see the front of the car from the driver's seat, just the tops of the wings, and visibility to the rear is non-existent except through the large rear view mirror and those on the doors.

Starting the engine is simple; pump the throttle several times to prime all those Webers, depress the clutch pedal and turn the key half way. A whir from somewhere behind your ears indicates the fuel pumps are working. Turn the key further and the starter spins the engine, sounding rather as if all the plugs are out; it's a constant-pitch whine because the cylinders are so well balanced. Only a couple of seconds are needed before it fires cleanly and reliably on all twelve; a marvellous, busy sound. 'Blip' the throttle to 2000rpm for a few seconds to circulate the engine oil and let up the clutch to get the gearbox working; it's very stiff when all that lubricant is cold.

The gearchange is well defined by the slotted gate. There's a detent on reverse (forward and left) which must physically be displaced before that gear can be engaged.

Throttle response is instantaneous and the revs drop immediately to tick-over once you take your foot off the pedal. It's a fairly stiff action, too, which needs concentration and the clutch is monumentally heavy. Depress it, move the lever back and left into first and you're ready to move off.

Trickling down the road, the revs rise rapidly, and you are soon reaching for second, which requires care in selection. All the while the magnificent sound of the twelve cylinders, four cams and countless chains and pulleys, fills your ears. The engine pulls so smoothly and without fuss; there's no hesitation while it warms up, a process which is surprisingly quick.

Even while the engine is cold it is quite clear that this is a car with immense dynamic capability. The steering is razor sharp, if heavy, and the brakes inspire enormous confidence. The massive discs and pads need plenty of warming up, though, and the pedal still needs a hefty shove even when they are at the correct temperature.

With the engine warm, the chance to use the performance presents itself. The speed at which the revs rise under full throttle is astounding and has one grabbing the gears almost as quickly as is possible. The faster the changes, the easier the shift becomes: the lever flicks through its gate in a most positive and satisfying way. The engine takes on a hard note under vivid acceleration and rises to a breathtaking howl near the top of the rev range, a sound so characteristic of a classic thoroughbred V12. It is easy to see why the passenger's footwell is equipped with a solid bar running across it – something to brace yourself against during acceleration and braking.

Once moving quickly, the Countach becomes easier to drive. The dead weight goes from the steering, the gearbox becomes more positive and the engine responds wonderfully precisely to the driver's commands. The lack of visibility to the rear ceases to be so much of a problem and one can feel the car become alive and begin to get into its stride.

There's no doubt that the performance is stunning. How many other road cars are capable of overtaking a flat-out Lotus Esprit Turbo before changing up into top gear? And how many other supercars can match the Countach's overtaking capability? 50-70mph in second gear takes a mere 1.9 seconds, while further up the speed range, 100-120mph takes just 4.3 seconds in fourth gear .... Small wonder the Countach is billed as the world's fastest production road car.

From a practical point of view it is hard to imagine using the Countach as anything other than a driving machine. With its impossible rear vision and the sheer brute force needed to manoeuvre the car in a tight situation, town driving could become an embarrassing proposition. Even though the engine feels marvellously tractable and fuss free, extended use in heavy traffic would soon cause it to lose its edge – hardly surprising with its high state of tune. I've no doubt there *are* people around the world who do use their cars for commuting but it is far more at home on the open road, being driven as intended – hard and fast.

All too quickly my test run was over. I'd just about got used to driving the car smoothly and making the most of that glorious engine. The controls are weighted such that one has to have a lot of stamina and strength to cope. The clutch, gearshift, steering, accelerator pedal action – all are very heavy but delightfully satisfying once in use. It's an addictive sensation having all that power under one's right foot. One feels the *need* to use it all the time.

Coming to a halt and switching off, the engine stops instantly, with no temperamental running on. The sound just ceases as there's no inertia to keep the engine spinning for those few revolutions after the ignition is cut. The marvellous noise behind you has gone and all that is audible is the soft ticking of the exhaust pipes as they cool. Open the door and it hisses up on its gas strut letting a blast of cold air enter the cabin.

So that's it. I've experienced the Countach, a sensation not many people are privileged enough to have. Outrageous, impractical and anything but sensible it may be, but currently it is surely the king of the supercars. Long live the Countach!

Main picture. Pictured at the factory in 1973, a pre-production Countach LP400. (Autocar/*QPL*)

Insert. The same car viewed with the lights in the 'on' position. The glass panel immediately ahead of the main light pods houses the sidelights and indicators, while a pair of fog/spot lamps are situated in the nose. Note the early frontal treatment on this car – no moulded spoiler yet. (Autocar/*QPL*)

Main picture. Pictured at the factory in 1973, a pre-production Countach LP400. (Autocar/*QPL*)

In the factory, a painted Countach received its wheels and final finishing touches back in 1973. Just visible are the two distributors fitted to this car, an early LP400. (Autocar/QPL)

The sight that must have stirred many hearts back in 1973. The door opening method is still unique today. Note that this car has factory 'PROVA' number plates, as this was a pre-customer car photographed by Autocar magazine editor, Ray Hutton, in 1973. (Autocar/QPL)

An early Countach LP400 showing the purity of line as Bertone saw it. Purposeful and elegantly simple it has yet to acquire the 'macho' look of the developed machine.

The factory service department. This Countach is seen without the rear wing.

A line of Countach bodies awaits finishing at the factory.

Two views of the 3929cc Lamborghini V12. The additional component located in the rear offside corner is the optional air-conditioning compressor.

In the paint shop. The finishing touches are being applied to a new Countach.

A 1985 model Countach LP500S; a sinister looking beast in all black colour scheme.

Finished and awaiting delivery at the factory, a new Countach poses in front of the whitewashed walls of the factory.

Above left. Interior of a 1982 Countach LP400S has relatively spartan trim, though bucket seats are comfortable. The cabin is deceptively spacious – for two people only, of course!

Above right. The interior had the 'pod' like instrument binnacle right from the start. Much use was made of suede as a trim material which gave the interior a more claustrophobic look than it could have had. Note also that this car has the fully adjustable steering which is a feature of today's cars. (Autocar/QPL)

Opposite. A mixture of shapes and curves that define the car's purpose – speed.

Below left. Rear lights of the Countach are set in reflective plastic surround.

Below right. The intake duct on the rear wing through which the radiator can be seen clearly.

Insert: Evolution is shown in this picture of Barry Robinson's 1983 LP500S. The overall shape remains but there are changes, most notable the extended wheel arches, front spoiler and, of course, that vast rear wing. The road wheels are different, too, and the passengers now have more window to wind down when it gets too hot!

The Countach LP500S pictured in perhaps its most aggressive pose.

ROAD TESTS

MOTOR week ending October 13, 1973

COUNTACH-LAST OF THE SUPER CARS?

It started as a one-off show-piece which worked unexpectedly well. Pete Coltrin describes how Lamborghini turned it into the world's most expensive—and maybe fastest—production car

When the Lamborghini LP 500 Countach first appeared at Geneva in March 1971 it was billed as an "idea" car—a joint Lamborghini-Bertone exercise. Aside from the many styling innovations the most interesting point was that its V12 engine was mounted longitudinally. Two years later a new Countach appeared at Geneva. Outwardly it was quite similar to the prototype but underneath it was quite different and no longer an idea car but a car scheduled for production later in the year—September, hopefully. It was fitting that both cars should be presented at Geneva. The Geneva Salon has always been Lamborghini's favourite springboard for presenting new cars: the first production 350 GT in 1964, the Miura in 1966, the Marzal in 1967, the Espada and Islero in 1968 and the Jarama in 1970. Of these only the Marzal didn't go into production though it is still used occasionally for demonstrations.

By 1971 the Miura, having exceeded even its makers' expectations, was getting on a bit (though it still had more than another year of production life to go) and Ingegnere Paolo Stanzani, Lamborghini's plant manager and head engineer, was obviously thinking of a replacement. And it seems most probable that these thoughts centred around a mid-engined car with the engine placed north to south, because of the study and expense involved in designing and building a transverse configuration. Detroit, Stuttgart and Turin can afford design exercises like these but it is pretty dear for a small firm. (The Marzal was an exception but casting "half a twelve" wasn't a prohibitive expense.)

Whether the Countach shape would be the package was not decided at that point. The Bertone body, at first appraisal, didn't seem practical for street use and many accepted it as another "fuori serie" or one-off show car. The "aerospace" cockpit, while incorporating many worthwhile ideas, seemed (and subsequently proved) to be even less practical. But the good points were there. Primarily the good aerodynamic shape of Bertone designer Gandini's body. The upward tilting doors, carefully counterweighted on assisting hydraulic struts, was obviously another good idea. Visibility to the rear was partially solved by a periscope-type rear view mirror concealed in the roof, and a shallow rear window. Accessibility to the engine was also quite reasonable.

Whether Bertone envisioned the shape as a production proposition is not known. Like Lamborghini, they didn't know at that point in early 1971. The rather light-hearted name Countach given to the car during the last minute rush at Carrozzeria Bertone before Geneva is an indication of this. Countach is a hard-to-define Piemontese expletive—let's leave it at that.

Up to this point Lamborghini has confined most of the mechanical expense to the engine, gearbox and driveline. The engine displaced 4971 cc with an 85 mm bore and a 73 mm stroke (compared to the 3929 cc V12 with a bore and stroke of 82 x 62 mm). This increase and the new sump meant a new block casting with ribbed lower flanks for strengthening. As indicated, the gearbox and drive train—since refined in detail—entailed the most thought and expense. For these reasons and because the car was primarily a show car the chassis was a rather simple and straightforward affair,

basically made up of square tubes with welded-in steel panels. In combination with the steel body it was called a "monocoque", though "semi-monocoque" is a closer description.

Front and rear suspensions were modified Lamborghini production car units. That the car was not only for show was soon evident. It ran and as soon as the car returned to Sant'Agata road testing began.

The "idea" car with its relatively unsophisticated chassis handled better than expected, it was quite manageable and had good weight distribution. Bob Wallace, Lamborghini's chief tester and development mechanic, was soon pounding up and down the roads between Bologna and Firenze (Florence) which comprise the old Mugello Circuit and include the Futa and Raticosa passes. Other testing was later conducted at the Modena and Varano tracks. Often the passenger would be either Stanzani or Ing. Massimo Parenti, a capable young engineer taking notes from a "Telemax" thermocouple—heat recording—"black box" or conducting wool-tuft air-flow tests. The car's shape was also working out well, with less tendency to lift than the early Miuras (in fact a bit too much negative lift at the front) and, as predicted, less sensitivity to side winds, due to more even weight distribution.

These first tests so impressed the staff at Lamborghini that it was decided to follow through with the Countach concept rather than pursue any other parallel ideas about a car to supersede the Miura—and doubtless there were other ideas if only in the pencil and paper stages. In May of 1972 Wallace and Stanzani had a trouble-free—and very fast—run to and from Sicily at Targa Florio time. After that trip the production of a Countach was no longer in doubt. While the prototype continued to be tested the design and engineering staff got busy on the new Countach which, in effect,

was to be an almost completely new car.

The firm's co-owners, Ferruccio Lamborghini and Georges Rossetti Stanzani, set down certain guide lines for the new "super" car. First and foremost Stanzani said it would be a true "macchina sportiva stradale"—neither a GT car nor a race car but a car guaranteed to do, among other things, a standing kilometre in 23 seconds or less. It would combine performance with comfort. Performance here was defined as a high power to weight ratio, stability and manoeuvrability. Comfort meant habitability, with heat and noise insulation, accessibility and dependability. None of these qualities could be neglected, each had to have a well thought out approach and solution. The car would not be built to a price. As far as was practicable, cost would be no object to achieve the aims although, as with all things, the line has finally to be drawn somewhere. The car would be sold only to discerning customers, known to the factory—serious enthusiasts who would appreciate such a car and know how to use it. A prestige car certainly by its very nature, but not for "status symbol" seekers. Too many of the latter gave the Miura a somewhat tarnished reputation—like pop stars who made headlines by crashing as many as three Miuras and others whose lines of "business" didn't exactly enhance the Miura image. The Countach, says Stanzani, is a car for the true enthusiast who will put up with certain inconveniences and do without minor amenities, such as limited luggage space and no electric window winders (impossible anyway). Provision is made for air conditioning but Lamborghini will be more than happy if no one ever asks for it (the weight penalty and a 10-15 bhp penalty makes them wince).

So much thought, study and—again—expense has gone into weight saving,

MOTOR week ending October 13, 1973

almost an obsession with Stanzani (elektron castings substituting for aluminium wherever possible, aluminium for steel, etc), that not many "extras" are going to be offered. Stanzani admits that the car is, in his words, "exaggerated" and makes no bones about it. That's the kind of car it is meant to be! Functional but by no means stark. Overall quality and finish are to be first class.

Lamborghini hope to build 30 to 50 cars per year and they already have a year's order book filled—including orders for at least two competition versions. At an estimated price of over 18,000,000 lire, in Italy, price is seemingly no problem.

"What", Stanzani was asked, "are some of the problems?" Sorting out the teething problems all new cars are prone to is first on the agenda. Keeping the car as light as possible another. The main problem, however, as far as production goes, is finding versatile, skilled craftsmen. People capable of building what will virtually be a handmade automobile. A prime example cited is the shortage of artisans who can shape metal. Not only body panels, which in the case of the Countach will be done in a special department at Bertone, but items such as the aluminium water expansion tanks which are hand made. This, not demand, will determine how many cars can be built.

ENGINE AND TRANSMISSION

Lamborghini cite numerous advantages for the fore and aft positioning of the V12 engine with the gearbox mounted ahead of the engine. Foremost is weight distribution. The longitudinal layout is claimed to give better directional stability compared to, say, the Miura, because the mass is closer to the centre of gravity and the aerodynamic pressure centre. Tests with both the prototype and the pre-production Countach bear this out, though better body aerodynamics enter into this as well. Aside from weight distribution the forward mounting of the gearbox is a particularly neat solution for a mid-engined road car. It obviates a long gear shift linkage and provides a direct, positive, gear change. It

also permits use of the basic front engine 12-cylinder block, turned back to front. This in turn facilitates future engine development for both types of car. (It is no secret that Lamborghini are working on larger displacement engines for future cars to help meet new anti-pollution standards.) The back-to-front layout offers other advantages. From a service standpoint it provides much better accessibility to the distributors, alternator, water pumps and compressor as well as facilitating timing chain adjustments.

Power is transmitted from the end of the crankshaft via a Fichtel and Sachs clutch (similar to the Porsche 917 unit) to the all-synchro five-speed indirect drive gearbox. From the secondary shaft drive is transmitted to the propeller shaft via a drop gear. This final drive shaft runs back through the engine sump to the differential, which has a ZF limited slip unit. The driveshaft runs in two roller bearings and is sealed off from the sump by oil seals to ensure separate lubrication for the gearbox and differential. The final drive ratio is determined by the drop gear rather than by varying ring and pinion ratios. The sump and differential housing is a single finned elektron casting with separate compartments.

After preliminary tests in 1971 with the prototype the five litre was replaced with a four litre version of the "twelve." The pre-production car is also running presently with the 3929 cc engine rather than the 4971 cc version. One reason is that the five litre engine is still not finalized—various modifications and variations are still being tested and studied. Most of these would appear to be experiments concerning porting and cam designs, valve sizes, air filters, and so on. Stanzani has let it be known, however, that titanium connecting rods are being considered.

There's another important reason for the

four litre engine being used till now. It isn't yet known whether the Italian transport ministry will consider the five litre as an enlarged version of the four litre, or whether they will treat it as a "new" engine thereby obliging Lamborghini to go through a lot of time-consuming test procedures and red tape. Hopefully this won't be necessary.

In either form the Countach block is easily recognized by the waffle-like strengthening ribs on the lower block surrounding the crankshaft. This is mostly to ensure adequate stiffness when the block is combined with the long sump/differential casting. The production Countach V12 has two six-cylinder Marelli distributors driven off the end of the left intake and exhaust cams. The end of the right hand head is machined and tapped to accept an air conditioner pump (if you insist). Instead of the now normal two alternators used on production Lamborghinis and the prototype 112 the production Countach has one heavy-duty 70 amp 114-volt Bosch alternator driven by a toothed belt which in turn is driven from the end of the crankshaft. The alternator is mounted on a small detachable subframe aft of the engine.

Carburation for either engine, four or five litres, is by six horizontal Weber twin choke 45 DCOE 23 carburettors. The pressurized cooling system uses two copper radiators. These are forward facing, mounted vertically and flanking the sides of the engine, with a cross-over connecting system. Air enters at the sides of the body through hip high intakes and NACA ducts and exits aft via slotted grilles atop the flat planed "fender" surface. Behind both radiators is an electrically driven fan; one is automatically controlled by a thermostat and the other is manually controlled from the cockpit. The radiators, just aft of the side mounted alloy 60 litre fuel tanks allow good weight distribution and proximity to the centre of gravity. It also allows shorter

MOTOR week ending October 13, 1973

water hoses and "plumbing" and lessens the likelihood of coolant loss. Another advantage of this location is that it avoids the influx of exiting hot air into the driving compartment. An oil radiator is located within the leading edge of the right front fender.

CHASSIS AND BODY

The biggest departure from the prototype Countach is the chassis of the production car. The prototype was built up—rather hastily—of square tubes and welded steel panels which with the steel body formed a "semi-monocoque" structure. It was a comparatively simple structure which served its basic purpose—that of a mobile test bed—well enough. However, for the production car Stanzani wanted maximum "leggerezza" (lightness) combined with better rigidity. He decided on a multi-tubular frame and a non-stressed aluminium body. Aside from weight and stiffness other factors in the decision for a multi-tubular frame were safety and maintenance inspection. One look at the frame indicates one of the reasons for the high price tag. The impressive structure is said to look more complicated than it really is but, admittedly, a good thump could be pretty expensive—though less so probably than a bent monocoque.

The Bertone two-place berlinetta body is of very thin gauge aluminium—less than one millimetre thick. Aside from the weight factor, aluminium, compared to steel, saves space. At one point during the planning stages avional was considered as a body material but here the cost really does get steep and outside the aviation industry it is next to impossible to find anyone with facilities, or the capability, for such construction. Some of the inner panels are, however, of avional where shape and form permit. The rest are of aluminium. The non-stressed body is riveted to the tubular frame. On the pre-production car normal "Vecris" glass is used all around. The series cars may use thin, light, Belgian "Gleverbel" glass.

A potential problem occurred to the designers concerning the upswinging doors —which work easily and well by the way. The problem was how you would get out if the car landed on its roof. In this unhappy event driver and passenger have access to two one-inch pins with hand grenade-like pull rings. These are located at the latch and hinge sills. Pulling these pins out and flipping over centre latches releases the door which should then fall off. (The designers toyed with the idea of using aircraft type explosive bolts to blow the doors off but that solution seemed a bit drastic.)

Both the steering wheel and the driver's seat are adjustable. Instruments are US Stewart Warner dials. Two rather thick stalks extending from either side of the steering column control the lights, indicators, wipers, washer, horn, etc. Other rocker switches are located on the centre console.

The spare wheel is located under the front lid. There is no pretence of bumpers capable of passing US regulations. Lamborghini is not concerning itself with the American market, at least for now (probably never) with this car.

SUSPENSION AND BRAKES

The front suspension is by unequal length A arms with coil spring/damper units and a stabiliser bar located behind the suspension. The rear suspension is by a single transverse upper link and a lower A arm with its apex attached to the frame, while two radius arms run forward and are also attached to the frame. There is also a stabiliser bar at the rear. Two shock/damper units per wheel are employed at the rear. The shock absorbers are lightweight Koni units with aluminium cylindrical bodies and are fully adjustable for bump and rebound. Front and rear hub carriers are elektron castings.

Girling four-piston dual-circuit disc brakes with alloy calipers are used. The discs are ventilated. This is a new Girling unit being used on the Countach for the first time. In the words of one of the Girling consultant engineers they are "a direct contribution from the competition department". Almost the first on-the-road tests of the new Countach concerned the brakes. These and subsequent track tests have found the new brakes very satisfactory

Attention to maintaining correct suspension settings, especially at the rear, is going to be of the utmost importance with these cars. More so than with the Miura probably. On the latter it was all too often neglected or set up improperly away from the factory which often led to grief. Properly set up and maintained there is no question in the minds of the engineers or Bob Wallace that the handling and roadability of the Countach is clearly superior to that of the Miura and, naturally being biased, to that of other contemporary cars. The rack and pinion steering is a Lamborghini unit housed, again, in an elektron housing. Stanzani has gone about as far as he can for a road car in weight saving, other elektron parts including the sump, wheel uprights, engine mounts, cam covers, oil pump housing, oil filter housing, rack and pinion housing, hand brake calipers, gearbox and clutch housings and wheels.

Super Profile

COUNTACH
continued

Who said the gull-wing door was dead—but it's an odd opening action. Note air scoops behind the door, and on the flanks

Above : the massive tubular chassis—note heavy side-members.
Left : super-sophisticated recording equipment used during high-speed trials. Left : a mass of carbs and camshafts under the central bonnet flap.
Below : limited luggage space in the tail

52

AUTOCAR w/e 8 June 1974

I SHOULD have realized that it would take more than an economy-imposed 100kph speed limit to hold down the talian enthusiasm for fast and beautiful cars. We were rushing through the lanes around Sant'Agata Bolognese. The speedometer flashed up to 220kph. There is a cluster of houses ahead —and a clear road beyond. The acceleration continues, to the accompaniment of the raucous, marvellous noise of a V12 on full song. The people who live in the outskirts of Modena are used to seeing exotic cars "on test". But this one still makes them stop in their tracks, stare, smile and wave in encouragement. When it appears at the electric gate at the entrance to the Lamborghini factory, necks crane from office

success and demand was such that it had to go into production before it had been developed to the level that its instigators wished.

The Countach is different; very different. Its V12 engine is mounted longtitudinally with the gearbox *in front* of it protruding into the cockpit from behind, presenting the gear lever to the driver in the same way as does a front-engined car, and transmitting its power through a prop shaft passing in a tube through the engine's sump to the differential. One can argue the pros and cons of such an arrangement from an accommodation point-of-view (the gearbox takes a lot of cockpit space) but it achieves the weight distribution (43:57 front to rear), centre of gravity, and general low-line configuration that the designers sought.

and sees it as the ultimate in that he can't imagine Lamborghini—or anyone else—will ever build another car of this type.

The Countach has certainly had time to evolve. It was first exhibited as the LP500 at the 1971 Geneva Show, but only during my visit in March this year was the first production version being completed. Now production is under way, though since the cars are hand-built—and complex—it isn't exactly a high volume assembly line. In fact Lamborghini expect to make four or five Countachs a month (compared to five Urracos and four front-engined V12s a week). Engine and transmission parts for an initial batch of 50 cars have been made; I understand that virtually all of these have been sold.

better compromise between rigidity, weight and badly needed interior space. "It had to be complex, to keep the weight down," explains Wallace, who tells me that the tubular frame weighs about 65kg (143lb). The original prototype had a 5-litre V12 engine but that proved too fragile in testing. Then they worked on a 4.4-litre version, but finally settled for the same dimensions and capacity (3,929 c.c.) as the other V12 models in the Lamborghini range. The water radiators were mounted longtitudinally at each side of the engine originally and fed with air from flush louvred ducts behind the side windows. This arrangement turned out to be inadequate in the first running tests and so now the radiators are mounted transver-

Supercars
-the end of the line?

Production of the £16,314 Lamborghini Countach has just got under way. Will speed limits, tightening legislation, and the lack of opportunity to use its 180mph performance make it the last of its type?

By Ray Hutton

windows and people come out specially to take another look at the most dramatic supercar of them all—the Countach.

Countach is a Piedmontese exclamation of astonishment, wonder and amazement. It is a singularly appropriate name for a no-holds-barred design, the objective of which was simply to produce the ultimate road car. Not just the fastest car ever designed for road, as opposed to racing use, but one which combined ultra-high speed with comparable standards of roadholding, handling, reliability, comfort, and style. The solutions reached by Lamborghini's design team (and since the celebrated Gian Paolo Dallara left them, they insist that a department rather than an individual is responsible for the design work) are radical. Faced with the same dilemma as Ferrari had in producing the Boxer BB (described in detail in *Autocar* 25 May, 1974), they chose a new arrangement for a mid-engine car. In the Boxer the flat-12 engine sits above the transmission which, although compact, results in a relatively high centre of gravity. The Lamborghini Miura had its V12 engine mounted transversely with the transmission similarly cross-ways in the car. Though the Miura was an "ultimate" car when first shown in 1966 it was a compromise in several respects. Its extrovert styling made it a tremendous

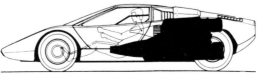

LINEA MONTAGGIO N° 1

COUNTACH

Bob Wallace, the self-effacing New Zealander who does Lamborghini's test driving and has worked on every model since the tractor manufacturer decided to "do a Ferrari" in 1963, holds the Countach as his personal favourite. He says that it is better than the Miura in every respect,

The overall concept and the general shape remain the same, but the production Countach is very different from that first prototype. At first the chassis had a sheet metal monocoque centre section including the floor pan. Now it has a complicated tubular space frame which provides a

Countach layout – mid-engined with the gearbox ahead of the engine. Weight distribution is near ideal; driver sits unusually far forward

sely, still in the amidships position but sticking out into the airstream and shrouded by conventional scoops with electric fans drawing air through them. About 30 per cent of the air to the radiators enters via NACA ducts newly added to the body sides.

It was intended to give the Countach a very futuristic facia layout centred, aircraft-style, around warning lights, with instruments only for second line diagnosis, not monitoring. That has been changed to a much more conventional arrangement of small dials contained in a narrow binnacle, heavily hooded to cut down reflections in the long, sharply angled windscreen. The production car differs from the prototype in many other details, including the line of its bodywork, though it has stayed free of the lips, spoilers and trim tabs that many predicted would be necessary to ensure safe stability towards its racing-type maximum speed.

Lamborghini do not know what that maximum speed is, which further underlines the difficulty of finding somewhere to achieve getting on for 200mph in controlled conditions. Wallace took the second prototype (modified to the mechanical specification of the production car) to Fiat's private 5km stretch of *autostrada* outside Turin and recorded 290 kph (180.2mph) at 7,600rpm in

Supercars –the end of the line?

top. He is sure that given a long enough run-in it would pull 7,800 so the magic 300kph (186.4mph) is obviously on the cards, even if 200mph (the original target of the advertising people, if not the engineers) is not. Wallace isn't very interested in its top speed now; he is confident that it can go faster than any customer is likely to want, and, more important, do so in safety. The aerodynamics must be good, for he reports that the car's behaviour remains consistent up towards its maximum. "The tail lightens up a bit over 250 (kph), but it's not excessive," he remembers cooly, "Maybe there is just a little too much downthrust at the nose." Startling acceleration, which he regards as a more usable quality, is indicated by the standing kilometre figure of 23.8 sec. It is proposed to offer two alternative final drive ratios, lower than the 4.09 to 1 fitted at present. "If you can't use the maximum, we might as well make the best of the acceleration," Wallace reasons.

I suspect that Wallace's Countach development programme has been less concerned with making it go than refining its roadholding, handling and braking. He has spent long hours at the Misano-Adriatico racing circuit sorting out the suspension. Though Lamborghini have never gone racing (that could change soon) Wallace has been around the Modena racing shops for 13 years and understands racing car construction techniques. A car with the performance of the Countach needs to lean heavily on racing design ideas. Thus it uses a fairly conventional racing suspension layout (though, like the Ferrari Boxer it has twin coil spring/ damper units at the rear to allow the drive shaft to pass between) and adjustable suspension ball joints. Those joints are specially made by Edenrich, run in nylon, and are sealed for life. The dampers look like Koni racing units but are in fact a special item with the aluminium racing casing but seals adapted for road use. Naturally, there are hefty anti-roll bars front and rear.

The brakes are massive racing-type ventilated discs with four-piston calipers made in aluminium and specially designed by Girling. To meet E-mark test requirements, small separate handbrake calipers have had to be added at the rear. Racing influence doesn't end there. The ZF self-locking differential is specially tailored for the car. "That's very important to the handling", says Wallace, "Sometimes those things can give very sudden effects." The wheels are 15in. diameter front and rear, but

7½in. wide at the front, 9½ at the back.

Even the clutch is a competition type component—an alloy-plate unit by Fichtel and Sachs similar to that developed for the Porsche 917.

The net result of all this has been to produce a car that has neutral handling characteristics up to impressively high limits, and then a gradual and—according to Wallace—easily controlled transition to final oversteer. The Countach corners with virtually no roll, brakes with scarcely any nose dip (some anti-dive is built into the suspension geometry) and yet rides well at anything above town speeds. The fuel is contained in two 14 gallon tanks at the centre of the car so that the balance does not change as the fuel load lightens.

The Countach certainly isn't an ordinary car to ride in. I went out with Wallace in the second prototype, which now differs from the customer cars in only a few details. At first it was disconcerting. It is ultra-low (42in. high); you sit (lie?) in a seat contoured to follow the natural line of the body. Thus the base of your spine is about the lowest point in the car while the seat "cushion" rises sharply under the knees. There is the illusion of sitting with one's knees higher than one's head, feet overhanging the front of the car. The seats are made from a lot of individual blocks of foam. Frankly, I found mine hard and uncomfortable, though Wallace says that the production ones are softer. My head touched the roof; he tells me that they have managed to find a few more precious centimetres in the cockpit of the final version. The seats, like the interior as a whole, are a tight fit. They locate you superbly thanks to the cushions' deep recesses, the wide body sills (conveniently at elbow height) to the outside and the massive central transmission tunnel. Though we went through the extremes of acceleration, braking and cornering—and there was no seat belt fitted—I stayed firmly in place, not even feeling a need to hold on to something.

The big windscreen is made of specially thin glass to prevent distortions. The view forward is superb, seemingly directly out to the road ahead. The screen and nose section are so steeply raked that one cannot see the front of the car from the reclined seating position. On the passenger side the facia falls away steeply, while in front of the driver there is a narrow deeply hooded instrument binnacle. All the interior in "number 2" is trimmed in dark brown suede to cut down reflections in the glass; there are still some however, notably of the demister ducts. The side windows are steeply curved too, though they have wind-down panels towards the trailing edges of the doors—not for ventilation but for paying autostrada tolls and so on. The doors themselves are real dream car stuff, pivoting forward like the wings of an insect. Their inspiration was the Carabo that designer Bertone first showed six years ago. They work very well once one remembers to push them upwards rather than outwards when getting out.

On the road

Perhaps the closest thing to the Countach in layout and the feeling of being attached to the front of a massive power unit is the Porsche 917 racing coupé. In the Countach, vibrations, rattles and so on have been eliminated, but there is a distinctly racing sound about it when the V12 is brought into life. The engine screams, the revs rise and fall in response to throttle bipping in a way that suggests a light flywheel. The gearlever is set high but close to the tiny and fully adjustable steering wheel. The gearbox has five speeds; the lever is gated and movements are long but very positive. Wallace slammed through the box from a standing start which was as notable for its lack of drama and wheelspin as it was for the accelerative g forces. He hurled the car through local lanes that he knows so well with the enthusiasm of an old Mille Miglia racer.

We returned to the factory where every available mechanic had been put to work on Countach number 3, the first production car which had to be ready for the Geneva Show in a few days' time. That one was at the final assembly stage but three others were at earlier stages of construction. The body, all aluminium alloy, is from a Bertone design but made at Lamborghini. Despite the thin

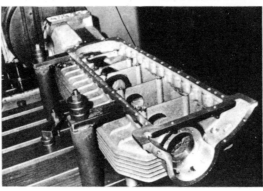

The Countach chassis (above) is a very complicated tubular spaceframe. Alloy body (below) is fashioned at Lamborghini and incorporates neat cockpit roll cage. The V12 engine is a special version for this car. Its magnesium sump (bottom) makes provision for drive shaft to pass through

screen pillars the cockpit contains a strong four-poster roll cage. The inner skins of the wings are glass fibre but the only part of the outer skin made of plastic is the front "bumper". That is designed to be replaceable in the event of light parking damage but there has been no attempt to meet American so-called safety regulations with this car; the Countach won't be sold in the United States.

It is amazing how much of the Countach is actually made at Lamborghini, or made outside suppliers specifically for this low-volume model. The lenses for the complex rear light units are one small example. "It wouldn't have looked right with something off a Fiat," justifies Wallace. This philosophy extends right through the design: What do we need to do the job? Can we build it? And—last on the list—how much does it cost? That is the reason why the Countach comes out at £16,314; its construction has been virtually no-expense spared.

A large number of the castings are magnesium, because the weight had to be kept down (the kerb weight is not much more than a 1,000kg—2,202lb). Lamborghini have a couple of Olivetti tape controlled machine tools so that they can machine batches of castings for each model in rotatation. It also allows them tremendous flexibility in component design. Thus, though the dimensions of the Countach's V12 are the same as that used in the Espada and Jarama, the pistons and crankshaft are the only shared

Headlamps (above) are built into electrically-operated "pop up" panels. Cockpit (below) is trimmed in non-reflective materials. Steering column is adjustable for height and reach. The second prototype (bottom) differs in a few details from the final version, though radiator ducting, changed several times during development, is now finalised

components between these models. The cylinder heads and camshafts are different, with the result that maximum power has increased to 385bhp (DIN) at 8,000rpm. The magnesium block has extra web-bings to cope with increased tor-que loading, while the sump casting (also magnesium) makes pro-vision for the aluminium tube to pass through containing the drive shaft from the gearbox to the differential.

The transmission is completely new, and of dry-sump type. Its housing is similarly beautifully fashioned in magnesium. Wallace pointed out to me the steel bearing inserts cast into the gearbox front cover and the magnesium sus-pension uprights: "It's not a racing car, so these things will not be thrown away after they have been taken off a couple of times."

Not a racing car. But a car capable of racing speeds and cor-nering power. Yet ability to afford one does not necessarily go hand-in-hand with the skill to drive such a potent machine. Does this pre-sent Lamborghini with a moral dilemma? The indications are, they say, that the Countach customers will be "more mature" than some of the sort of people who buy Espadas for their extro-vert good looks. "It's not a difficult car to drive," says Wallace, whose lengthy development programme has ensured that it meets the high standards that they set for themselves. "If this is the last car of its type ever to be made, we figure we should build it as best we possibly can . . . . ." □

Super Profile

On the road . . .

On the Road in a Lamborghini Countach

ALTHOUGH we covered the Lamborghini Countach in last month's Supercar comparison we thought borrowing a Lamborghini was rare enough to justify a closer look, and also to tie up with our sports car Buyers Guide. In fact, Lamborghinis shouldn't be that rare; according to the History of Lamborghini (published by Transport Bookman) — Rob Box and Richard Crump compiling the collection of pictures and specifications that make up most of the book — the production figures for 1963–73 of some 19 separate models (including five one-offs) was 3187, of which the most popular have been the first Espada (920) and the Miura in all its forms at 900. Obviously, it is because there aren't that many in the UK, that one regards the cars as rare. Part of the reason for this has been the fluctuating fortunes of Lamborghini importers, but these are now established with Berlinetta Italia Ltd., 189 Godstone Road, Whyteleafe, Surrey under Roger Phillips as sole importers; Maltins of Henley are main sales and service dealers with Portman Garages as sales dealers, plus a handful of service dealers of whom Bugatti specialists, Tula Engineering, are one.

Although the Countach which appeared in 1971 was the logical successor to the Miura which was first seen in chassis form in 1965, the two cars are very different; points of similarity are the 3939cc V-12 and the hand of Bertone in the styling. The Miura used a sort of holey monocoque chassis entirely constructed of sheet steel — where others might have used tubes fore and aft of the centre section, Lamborghini used fabricated sheet steel box sections with holes punched in two faces. The V-12 was slung transversely immediately behind the cockpit bulkhead with the gearbox effectively just behind the sump and part of it.

The Countach was first shown as a five-litre at Geneva in 1971 but it wasn't really until 1974 that production got under way with the four-litre. The chassis for this was a multi-tube space frame — like that of Mr Ferrari's rival Boxer — but the V-12 had been turned through 90° to run longitudinally. To keep the weight distribution less tail-heavy, the gearbox was mounted in front of the engine with the prop-shaft running back through the sump to a final drive unit; although this jacks the engine up, raising the centre of gravity, it gives a good distribution of the masses with no mechanical overhang behind the rear wheels, which leaves a useful space for luggage. Whether the resultant low polar moment of inertia is still regarded as being as desirable as it was in 1971 is another question, as the Grand Prix scene rejected the theory — only March tried it with the gearbox behind the engine but ahead of the rear wheels — at about the time the Countach appeared. It makes for quick and accurate handling from quick and accurate drivers, but they preferred the lazier response characteristics of the higher polar moments.

Bertone built the aluminium bodies to start with, but Lamborghini took this over in March 1974 as production got under way, the successful crash test taking place at MIRA on 21 March, 1974. The original LP500 had been a very clean wedge with the radiator intakes, just aft of the rear door, recessed with little guide vanes; outlets were into the hopefully low pressure area of the engine cover surrounded by rear window and rear wing flying buttresses. By the time the LP400 came into production, the intakes had become scoops almost totally masking visibility through newly-added corner windows; outlets had moved to the top of the outer rear surfaces and NACA ducts had been sculpted behind the doors. Using contrasting colours for ducts and outlets heightens the additional nature of the changes, but doesn't stop the car being still a real head-turner.

Suspension follows double-wishbone and coil spring practice with the brakes using ventilated discs all round. The 60° V-12 has four chain-driven overhead camshafts, six 42 DCOE Webers and produces 375bhp at 8000rpm and 266lb. ft. at 5000rpm.

As I recounted before, the visibility forwards takes some getting used to with nothing apparently in front of the base of the screen; sideways, it is acceptable and the thin bar across the side window where it opens doesn't obtrude; three-quarter rear view is non-existent; to the rear the tunnel slot arrangement provides light on the mirror which gives a reasonable view dead aft. Such factors are all very noticeable when you first get in the car, but it doesn't take long to get used to placing the car and arranging your driving according to the visibility limitations — lane changing on a busy motorway requires a memory for the cars that have moved into the blind spot, which an external driver's mirror doesn't fully uncover.

The engine sounded fine, and had a really useful performance band, although I was never tempted to go beyond 6500rpm let alone the remaining 1500rpm before peak power is theoretically produced — it just began to sound strained and feel breathless and there was still plenty of performance in the next gear.

Lamborghini make their own gearbox and final drive; as you sit virtually on the box you can hear the drop gears whining when the oil is cold in lower gears, but this soon disappears and is, anyway, less obtrusive on later cars. Despite the short linkage run it was still a rather stiff lever movement, but positive and direct.

What I was particularly pleased to find was that the chassis is so well sorted for road use; it would take surface breaks without sending bonks shuddering through the structure, it rode well over humps and hollows and at speed it was impressively stable with strong gusting side winds scarcely discernible. It went round corners in a reassuringly roll-free and flat fashion with little departure from the chosen line with throttle movement. The chassis has obviously been well designed and developed.

Although it would be totally impractical as a commuter car it is certainly usable for long journeys and the boot space is excellent for the type of car — it will actually take suitcases. I was very grateful to Maltins and their customer for the chance to make the acquaintance of the Countach. Obviously it is a classic in the making and will justifiably take its place alongside the Miura and those earlier Touring-styled 350 and 400GT, of which there were some 135 and 250 produced respectively. You could also choose from 400 Jaramas or 225 Isleros. Present production includes the transverse V-8 mid-engined Urraco and the continuing Espada, alongside the Countach. It took me a few years to accept that a man who set out to tap the Ferrari market could actually do so, but Lamborghini is now a well and truly established manufacturer of fine Italian cars.●   **M.H.L.B.**

The Countach is striking from any angle. Gear lever gate is well defined. Front compartment contains spare wheel, brake units, battery, etc.

Auto TEST

Lamborghini Countach 500 S
King of the Supercars?

WELL BEFORE one learns what is under that extraordinary Bertone bodywork, the shape of the Lamborghini Countach announces that here is something different, even by the other-world standards of the so-called "supercar." It is as unusual now as it was when it made its prototype bow at the 1971 Geneva Show. The doors are neither conventional nor 300 SL-style gull wing; each opens upwards, yes, but from a horizontal pivot at the front (so that unlike any other type of door, Countach ones do not require greater width than the car's in which to open). The radiators for engine cooling are not in the nose, but carried racing-car-fashion, one each side behind the cockpit, fed by a combination of lower NACA-type intakes and part of the big rectangular ducts, reminiscent of jet intakes on Mach 2 supersonic military aircraft, which are such a distinctive feature of Countach upperworks.

Side intakes, which dominate appearance of car

Only the lower part of the horizontally split side windows open. Then there is the size; with a wheelbase (96½in.) which is no bigger than an Alfasud's, and an overall length of only 13ft 7in., the car is no less than 6ft 6¾in. wide — the same as a Rolls-Royce Phantom VI limousine.

The engine is the sort you might expect. Originally an 82×62mm 3,929 c.c. V12, its bore and stroke were increased at this year's Geneva Show to 85.5 × 69mm, taking the capacity to 4,754 c.c., and giving the car its new description of "LP 500S" (the badge on the back muddlingly adds a nought, making 5000 S). All aluminium-alloy cased, the engine has wet cylinder liners, a seven-bearing crankshaft, chain-driven twin overhead camshafts, six downdraught twin-choke Weber carburettors, twin Bendix electric fuel pumps, two electric fans and an oil cooler. This 375 bhp power unit sits conventionally (for a mid-engined car) longways, but its relationship with the transmission is most unusual; it lives between the five-speed gearbox and the final drive. The box is in front of the engine, driven directly off it, with a shaft which in effect extends the gearbox output one rearwards, under the crankshaft, to the pinion and crown-wheel, requiring the engine to be raised slightly.

As well as the 90-deg different layout, the Countach differs from the old Miura in that engine, gearbox and final drive are separately lubricated.

There is nothing unitary about the chassis and body. It is an elaborate multi-tubular space frame with no tube larger than 1¼in. diameter. The body is aluminium alloy, apart from the steel roof and the glass-fibre cockpit floor, cockpit interior and tunnel for the gearbox where it intrudes into the cabin. Coil springs are used for the all-independent suspension, laid out with 1960s-racing-car wheel location — double wishbone in fact in front and, in geometry, behind.

How does it differ from the LP 400 S? (still, incidentally, in production). The increase in engine capacity is accompanied by a reduced compression ratio (9.2 instead of 10.5 to 1), larger Webers (45 DCOE 142s instead of 40 DCOEs) and revised combustion chambers, which together give the V12 an allegedly less "peaky" power curve and correspondingly lower-peaking but 13.9 per cent greater maximum torque of 303lb ft at 4,500 instead of 5,500 rpm. Top gear is made longer-legged at 0.707 instead of 0.775 to 1, to take advantage of the higher gearing in both speed and economy.

Performance
Shattering

Autocar went to collect the test car from the world famous factory of what, since the last takeover, by Patrick Mimram, just over a year ago is called Nuova Automobili Ferruccio Lamborghini SpA, at the little town of Sant' Agata Bolognese near Modena. On arrival, we were somewhat horrified to learn that the only 500S available was a nearly brand new one, with only 239 kilometres (149 miles) on its mileometer. It was explained that whilst a Countach with 3,000 miles behind it would certainly be up to 500rpm faster in top speed, the considerable amount of engine bench running before installation ensured that the unit was at any rate initially run-in. Each V12 has six hours of being driven by an electric motor as its first breaking-in treatment. It is then started up and worked against a brake at various constant rpm between 2,000 and 6,000 in 1,000 rpm intervals, at 1½ to 2 hours for each speed, after which its maximum power and torque are measured to ensure that the engine is up to specification. Lamborghini are by no means a big company, especially now in their leaned-down, but apparently more efficient size, yet they have four fully equipped engine test houses in which this power unit preparation — two days of it — takes place.

Certainly, the test car's engine

Above: That most unusual of bodies seen from in front, displaying air intakes for brakes and interior (front) and engine (rear), the small headlamp flashing lamps and the distinctive doors

*Below, left: Only the bottom half of the horizontally split window opens
Below: Seen from the rear, the lack of over-shoulder vision is obvious*

Lamborghini LP 500S

One of Italy's immensely fast mid-engined supercars in its latest "500" form. Original production car had 3.9-litre V12, four ohc aluminium alloy, wet-linered engine arranged conventionally longways (in contrast to earlier transverse, mid-engined Miura). Since Geneva show this year, fitted with bored and stroked 4.75-litre version of engine, giving claimed 375 bhp at 7,000 rpm instead of at 8,000, and 302 lb.ft. torque at 4,500 rpm instead of 266 at 5,500 rpm. Space frame chassis, Bertone-styled aluminium alloy body. All-independent coil spring suspension — wishbone in front, wide based (old racing car style) at rear, steering rack and pinion, brakes ventilated outboard discs. Available in Britain in right-hand-drive.

PRODUCED BY:
Nuova Automobili Ferruccio Lamborghini SpA,
40019 S. Agata Bolognese,
Via Modena 12B, Italy

SOLD IN THE UK BY:
Portman Garages Ltd.,
101 George Street,
London W1

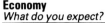

Autocar, w/e 9 October 1982

didn't sound or feel tight or in the least bit unwilling. In typically warm Italian summer weather, it starts easily after a prod or two of accelerator pumps and will trickle along without temperament or too much noise through built-up areas. But this is not a town car; it is for the open road, preferably clear of obstruction to the Countach's passage or forward vision. The engine, without being too noisy, is always entirely dominant in sound, and so dominant in performance. You don't call upon it to do anything important at below 10 mph in second, 30 in third, or 40 in the two uppermost gears; it is not enthusiastic about crankshaft speeds of less than around 1,700 rpm, so Countach trickling isn't the same as crawling lazily along in top gear in, say, a manual Rover V8.

Get on to that open road – the sun is just rising, the sky is cloudless, the air still, the *autobahn* straight and level for the next three lonely miles. Stop on the hard shoulder, choosing a place free from loose traction-spoiling chippings. Engage first, set the throttle so that the revcounter reads 5,000 rpm. A last scan of the instruments, and a look behind; all is clear. Let go of the clutch pedal, as if it had instantly become burning hot.

The surface under the wheels is undeniably grip-full, and the back tyres are Pirelli's lowest profile and, by road standards, extremely wide 345/35VR 15in. Yet they spin, just long enough to keep the engine revving marvellously on song as the crouching car rockets forward. The acceleration times tell the story as well as any words – 60 mph passes in 5.6sec, 80 in 8.8, 100 in 12.9, the quarter-mile in 14.0, 120 in 18.5 140 in 28.0 and 160 in 58.0, all within the space of little more

That superb engine; access is not as bad as it looks

than two miles. The rushing road is still clear as far as the eye can see, so you keep your right foot down until the revs stop rising in the 24.52 mph per 1,000 rpm fifth, at 164 mph - 6,700 rpm, with a still-young engine. Interestingly, the same maximum was obtained during homologation tests on the 2½ mile diameter NARDO track under "not ideal" conditions.

The gated gear change is not like the majority of today's ordinary saloons in weight; it requires more effort, but by no means too much, and it is pleasingly precise, almost machine-like in character. The clutch release pressure is high, at just under 50lb – that is around twice what is usual in lesser cars today – but it does its job very competently, in spite of the traction of those very large tyres, a ZF limited slip differential and a static distribution of unladen weight which is 56.1 per cent to the rear. Outside cities, the high pedal effort is unimportant, but

servo assistance would be no doubt welcomed with relief by Countach owners whose natural habitat is the town. Gear ratios are more or less conventionally spaced, apart from a curiously slightly less narrow gap between second and third than between first and second. This is shown by the speeds to which the engine drops on each upward change made at the same 7,000 rpm. First takes the car to 54 mph, revs dropping to 5,050 rpm on the change into the 75 mph second; second into the 112 mph third drops the speed to 4,700 rpm; third into the 141 mph fourth, to 5,550, and fourth to fifth, 6,000.

From just below 2,000 rpm onwards, the engine pulls superbly, with no hesitations or flat spots. Although by no means quiet, it is properly smooth by the standards of Italian supercars, and responds immediately to every movement of the throttle pedal. You can coax it away from 1,000 rpm, but this is not its *metier*, as one expects from such a car.

Gearlever is gated, with swing-away reverse protection. Instruments from left are ammeter, oil temperature, 200 mph speedometer with twiddle-zero trip, oil pressure, 9,000 rpm revcounter, water temperature and fuel. Stalks are conventional, and include horn. Centre panel deals with air conditioning and minor switches

Economy
What do you expect?

Although the less peak-y, more flexible larger engine has less thirst as one of its justifications, it cannot be pretended that fuel economy is a high priority in Countach design. The provision of twin 13.2 gallon tanks, one on each side, is one admission of this; they are replenished from separate fuel fillers each placed in a hatch in the NACA intakes behind the doors, and are joined by a small bore balance pipe, so that it is best to top up from both sides. We have no proper test experience of the smaller-engined Countach, but credible reports suggest it would return between 10 and 14 mpg. If that is so, the 500's 14.6 mpg in our hands – over a regrettably too short test mileage – suggests that there has been a worthwhile improvement. Nevertheless, we would be surprised if any owner buys the car with fuel saving in mind.

Noises
Magnificent ones

He will also not put quietness as an essential either; in fact, he may well be demanding some audible suggestion of the car's power. Lamborghini have in fact here done a clever job, balancing safely between the demands of the exhibitionist and those of the socially conscientious – bearing in mind in the latter case that even the Italian bystander tends to tolerate more noise from powerful cars than the majority of less Latin races. The engine makes a growl which most people who have anything to do with the car will thoroughly approve of. There seems little point in the provision of the Japanese-made Alpine Electronics stereo radio, except at low speeds. The engine is free of the clatter which is a feature that owners of older Ferrari V12s will be familiar with; there is a little gear whine, but not much. Road noise is understandably pronounced, as you might expect given the huge tyres fitted. Wind noise proved to be low, if one took the trouble to search for it by switching off the engine at speed; you don't hear it otherwise.

Road behaviour
Immense grip

The car is fitted with smaller section tyres at the front – 205/50VR15in. – as befits its layout (the spare is a skinny Michelin 105R18X on a correspondingly narrow rim, saving space in the front boot). The rack and pinion steering is reasonably appropriately geared, at 3.2 turns from lock to lock for a 38ft 7in. minimum turning circle diameter. It is on the heavy side, but beautifully direct and accurate, giving the sort of good response that such a car demands, yet without being in any way twitchy. There is good feel of what those squat low-profile front tyres are doing through the 13½in. diameter rim.

Straight stability at maximum speed is reassuringly good in spite of a suggestion of lightening steering. There is the added bonus of no hint of any sort of bump steer or suspension misbehaviour. This is obviously due to the classically laid out and excellently designed wheel location, which permits no improper excursions or wheel angles. This, the car's ideal weight distribution, and its typical mid-engine low polar moment of inertia are largely responsible for its wonderfully balanced cornering. There is just the right amount of understeer to preserve stability, and which predominates in a high speed bend most reassuringly. Use the throttle and a low gear in a slow bend and the tail can be powered out, pleasantly controllably, with no uncomfortable sharpness either on provoking such a slide or catching it. Roll is hardly discernible.

The Countach rides more absorbently than you might expect, but is obviously isn't a car to be taken over large bumps if one can avoid them. The big tyres do help somewhat in this respect, with their not-so-high pressures.

Performance like this machine's demands good brakes. The 500 S has them, in the shape of servo-assisted 11.8in. diameter front discs, and 11.1in. rears, all outboard, and all of the ventilated type. Couple these to those tyres, and that perfect weight distribution, and you have something closer than usual to modern racing car retardation. The pedal response starts off on the light and powerful side, with only 20lb pedal effort needed for 0.35g deceleration, continuing in virtually linear progression to just under 1g at 50lb. For many ordinary cars, especially with today's (in our view) wrong-headed insistence on never locking the

Above: Front boot has spare wheel and battery, brake cylinder, horns and air conditioning heat exchanger in it

Below: Rear boot is unexpectedly roomy

back tyres, so that braking systems are set too front-biased, this would be as far as one might get. This is not the limit with the Countach and its P7s, which returned 1.05g at 60lb and 1.1 at 70lb. The tyres and the dynamic weight distribution two-up are largely responsible for such an achievement of course, but there is also the excellent balance of the brakes to be thanked. Fade resistance is what it ought to be for such a car — competent. The handbrake acts on the back brakes, and typically of such cars, is not very effective.

Behind the wheel
Italian

The test car was finished in white, with matching white leather upholstery. One wondered about the practicality of this when clambering over the upholstered broad sill into the very well-locating hammock-like seat. One inside, shutting the hydraulically counterbalanced door by reaching up and slightly forward to the edge of the small pocket and pulling, one feels noticeably enclosed, although not too much so for a 6ft Briton, who has around half an inch of headroom. That size of driver has inadequate legroom, but the telescopic and rake-adjustable upper steering column in its uppermost setting allows just enough clearance of thighs in spite of the knees-up driving position, although heel-and-toe changes are very difficult, solely because of the right knee being obstructed by the steering wheel rim.

Only the bottom section of the side window winds down — not very convenient. At the *autostrada* toll booth, the experienced Countach driver opens the door instead of the window to pay his dues — no problem, with upward opening, no matter how close the side of the toll-collector's hutch.

In contrast to the unusual — some might say bizarre — exterior styling, the layout and design of instruments and controls are straightforward. The steering wheel is a pleasingly plain three-spoke, thick, leather-rimmed one. Six simple dials confront one ahead of it, just visible within the upper half of the wheel; the minor ones are ammeter, oil temperature, oil pressure, water temperature, oil temperature and fuel, whilst the 200 mph speedometer and 9,000 rpm rev counter take up the bigger dials. On the left-hand-drive car tested, the stalk control on the right is for wipe/wash and the left hand one deals with signalling, including — rather surprisingly on an Italian car — the air horns.

The water-valve heater and the standard air conditioning equipment are independent of each other; air conditioning makes up somewhat for the unusual lack of through-flow. The heater has three Fiat-style demister outlets, but the weather during the test period made any test of its effectiveness impossible.

Forward vision is as it should be, apart from the problems common to so many supercars with well-raked windscreens, of some reflections of the top of the dash, in spite of its darker finish. The flat glasses of the instruments also suffer from reflections. The view behind is what you might expect, intimidatingly blind, except dead aft, and even then only good provided you don't want to check anything not that far behind which is on the road. The Countach is not the world's most ideal car for traffic, because of its rear blindness, which is a very great handicap.

Living with the Countach

Oddment space inside the cockpit is limited to a glove cubby in front of the passenger, the narrow gap behind the seats into which thin things like, say, a slender map book can be squeezed, the handy door pockets (deeply lipped to stop things falling out on raising the door), and whatever you are prepared to put up with on the floor. Unlike several other mid-engined cars, the Countach makes up for this to some quite tolerable extent with its luggage space. There is some room for squashy items under the nose panel, providing that they are compatible with the thin spare wheel, air conditioning pipes, two frame cross tubes, horns, brake master cylinder and battery. The boot proper, behind the engine compartment, is really quite generous for this type of car, and capable of taking quite a useful amount of mostly non-rigid luggage.

The passenger seat footwell has a cross bar near its bottom which acts as a foot brace. Like the driver's, the passenger's seat gently forces a reclined posture with excellent sideways and lumbar support. Rake adjustment is not possible, but there is adjustment of the inclination of the entire seat, within limits.

Tucked into the back of the car with its neat pack of DCOEs breathing into the inside of each camshaft V, the twin radiators on

each side, and the distributor behind on the end of the left bank's exhaust camshaft, the engine is a delight to behold, although not easy to get at. It has the unusual (for a European market car) feature of an exhaust air pump as an anti-emissions measure. The belt drives for alternator, air conditioning compressor and air pump

Seating is lie-back and leather is used extensively

are not awkward to adjust, the oil filler is accessible at the rear of the right hand exhaust camshaft cover, whilst the large oil filter lies on its side close to the back.

Headlamps are pop-up type, electrically raised. For lamp flashing, the small rectangular spot lamps fixed in the front are used. A buzzer reminds you if you switch off, leaving headlamps on. There is just one wiper, which has a pantograph linkage.

The car tested was not fitted with the beautifully made, heavily cambered wing at the rear, because this reduces top speed, as you might expect.

Everything up: Countach with all hatches and lamps up

The Countach range

You can no longer get the earlier 4-litre LP 400; the more flexible LP 500 tested is sold in this country by Portman Garages in London and Denham, who retain the services of some key people, long-experienced with Lamborghini and its customers in this country. There are two prices; £49,500 in the condition tested, £50,644 with the spectacular-looking but retarding rear wing.

HOW THE LAMBORGHINI COUNTACH LP 500S PERFORMS

Figures taken at 200 miles by our own staff on the Continent.

All Autocar test results are subject to world copyright and may not be reproduced in whole or part without the Editor's written permission.

TEST CONDITIONS:
Wind: 0-3 mph
Temperature: 82 deg C (28 deg F)
Barometer: 30.90in. Hg (1,023 mbar)
Humidity: 95 per cent
Surface: dry asphalt and concrete
Test distance: 320 miles

MAXIMUM SPEEDS

Gear	mph	kph	rpm
Top (mean)	164	264	6,700
(best)	165	266	6,750
4th	152	245	7,500
3rd	128	206	8,000
2nd	85	137	8,000
1st	62	100	8,000

ACCELERATION

FROM REST

True mph	Time (sec)	Speedo mph	True mph	Time (sec)	Speedo mph
30	2.4	33	100	12.9	106
40	3.3	44	110	15.3	116
50	4.4	55	120	18.5	126
60	5.6	65	130	22.4	136
70	7.0	76	140	28.0	146
80	8.8	86	150	37.2	157
90	10.7	96	160	58.0	168

Standing ¼-mile: 14.0 sec, 105 mph
Standing km: 24.9 sec, 135 mph

IN EACH GEAR

mph	Top	4th	3rd	2nd
10-30	–	–	–	3.8
20-40	–	–	5.3	3.9
30-50	9.8	6.4	4.4	2.3
40-60	8.2	5.5	3.8	2.1
50-70	7.4	5.2	3.4	2.3
60-80	7.1	5.0	3.1	–
70-90	6.8	4.9	3.4	–
80-100	6.8	4.9	4.0	–
90-110	6.5	5.0	4.6	–
100-120	6.8	5.5	5.3	–
110-130	7.9	6.8	–	–
120-140	9.7	8.8	–	–
130-150	14.0	–	–	–
140-160	26.4	–	–	–

FUEL CONSUMPTION

Overall mpg:
14.6 (19.3 litres/100km)
3.21 mpl

Constant speed

mph	mpg	mpl	mph	mpg	mpl
30	21.0	4.62	70	17.7	3.89
40	20.2	4.44	80	16.7	3.67
50	19.3	4.25	90	15.8	3.48
60	18.7	4.11	100	14.0	3.08

**Autocar
formula:** Hard 13.1mpg
     Driving Average 16.1mpg
and conditions Gentle 19.0mpg

Grade of fuel: Premium, 4-star (97 RM)
Fuel tank: 26.4 Imp. galls (120 litres)
Mileage recorder reads: 2.0 per cent long

Official fuel consumption figures
Figures not available

OIL CONSUMPTION

(SAE 10W/40W) 400 miles/pint

BRAKING

Fade (from 105 mph in neutral)
Pedal load for 0.5g stops in lb

	start/end		start/end
1	25-20	6	38-35
2	25-20	7	38-35
3	27-20	8	35-35
4	30-25	9	35-35
5	34-30	10	35-35

Response (from 30 mph in neutral)

Load	g	Distance
20 lb	0.35	86 ft
30 lb	0.58	52 ft
40 lb	0.72	42 ft
60 lb	1.05	28.7 ft
70 lb	1.1	27.4 ft
Handbrake	0.14	215 ft
Max. gradient: 1 in 6		

CLUTCH
Pedal 48 lb; Travel 6¼in.

WEIGHT
Kerb, 26.0 cwt/2,913 lb/1,321 kg
(Distribution F/R, 43.9/56.1)
Test, 29.6 cwt/3,313 lb/1,503 kg
Max. payload: 412 lb/190 kg

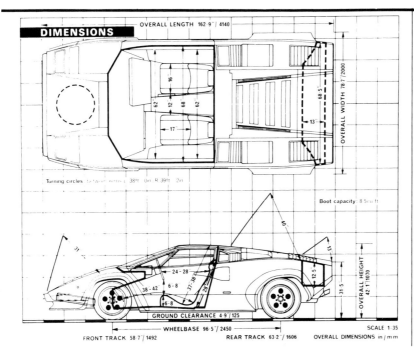

DIMENSIONS

OVERALL LENGTH 162·9″ / 4140

OVERALL WIDTH 78·7 / 2000

Turning circles between kerbs L 38ft 0in, R 39ft 2in

Boot capacity: 8.5cu ft

GROUND CLEARANCE 4·9″/125

OVERALL HEIGHT 42·1″/1070

WHEELBASE 96·5″/2450

FRONT TRACK 58·7″/1492   REAR TRACK 63·2″/1606   OVERALL DIMENSIONS in / mm

SCALE 1·35

PRICES

Basic	£39,732.45
Special Car Tax	£3,311.03
VAT	£6,456.52
Total (in GB)	**£49,500.00**
Seat Belts	Standard
Licence	£80.00
Delivery charge (London)	£250.00
Number plates	£25
Total on the Road (exc. insurance)	**£49,855.00**

EXTRAS (inc. VAT)
Rear wing   £1,144.25

TOTAL AS TESTED ON THE ROAD	**£49,855.00**

Insurance   on application

SERVICE & PARTS

	Interval
Change	6,000
Engine oil	Yes
Oil filter	Yes
Gearbox oil	Yes
Spark plugs	Yes
Air cleaner	Yes
Total cost	**£450.05**

(Assuming labour at £20.70/hour inc. VAT)

Parts prices not available at the time of going to press.

WARRANTY
12 months/12,000 miles

SPECIFICATION

ENGINE
	Mid, rear-wheel drive
Head/block	Al. alloy
Cylinders	V12, wet liners
Main bearings	7
Cooling	Water
Fan	Twin electric
Bore, mm (in.)	85.5 (3.37)
Stroke, mm (in.)	69.0 (2.72)
Capacity, cc (in.³)	4,754 (290)
Valve gear	4-ohc
Camshaft drive	Chain
Compression ratio	9.2-to-1
Ignition	Marelli electronic
Carburettor	6 horiz. Weber 45DCOE twin choke
Max power	375 bhp (DIN) at 7,000 rpm
Max torque	302 lb ft at 4,500 rpm

TRANSMISSION
Type	Five-speed
Clutch	Single dry plate

Gear	Ratio	mph/1000rpm
Top	0.707	24.52
4th	0.858	20.20
3rd	1.086	15.96
2nd	1.625	10.67
1st	2.232	7.77
Final drive gear	Hypoid bevel	
Ratio	4.091	

SUSPENSION
Front – location	Ind. wishbone
– springs	Coil
– dampers	Telescopic
– anti-roll bar	Standard
Rear – location	Ind. wide-based wishbone
– springs	Coil
– dampers	Twin telescopic
– anti-roll bar	Standard

STEERING
Type	Rack and pinion
Power assistance	None
Wheel diameter	13½ in.
Turns lock to lock	3.2

BRAKES
Circuits	Twin
Front	11.8 in. dia. vent disc
Rear	11.1 in. dia. vent disc
Servo	Vacuum
Handbrake	Centre lever, rear discs

WHEELS
Type	Campagnola al. alloy
Rim width	8½ in. front, 12 in. rear
Tyres – make	Pirelli
– type	P7 15 in.
– size	205/50VR front, 345/35VR rear
– pressures	F 33, R 36 psi (normal driving)

EQUIPMENT
Battery	12V 72Ah
Alternator	70A
Headlamps	220/220W
Reversing lamp	Standard
Electric fuses	16
Screen wipers	2-speed
Screen washer	Electric
Interior heater	Water valve
Air conditioning	Standard
Interior trim	Leather seats, nylon headlining
Floor covering	Carpet
Jack	Screw scissor
Jacking points	Under sills, one each side
Windscreen	Laminated
Underbody	Al. alloy body; glass fibre floor/ wheel arch

BUYING

The very nature of the Lamborghini Countach means that it is undoubtedly one of the rarest cars of any type in the world.

With under 1000 registrations since the car was first introduced more than 13 years ago, it is not surprising that the chances of seeing one on the road are pretty rare. For most people, the opportunity of actually being able to own one is merely a pipe dream, while those who do aspire to such cars more often than not have them in addition to other cars and therefore do not use them every day. To do so would surely be pushing practicality to its limit.

Every Countach is carefully registered by the factory as and when it is built and, because each is meticulously hand-made, it might be argued that every car is slightly different from its brother. That said, the standards of finish are of the very highest order with panel fit and paint quality making it very difficult indeed to tell any two cars apart.

Possible problem areas to look for on the Countach, as with any 'supercar' of this calibre, are the engine and drivetrain because, although they are engineered and built to the very highest standard, abuse from previous owners will undoubtedly lead to trouble, particularly from the clutch, the gearbox synchromesh and the engine valve gear. With unsympathetic use where the respective lubricants have not been allowed to warm through and circulate properly before full performance is used, wear will take place resulting in the possibility of enormous repair bills. Think in terms of many hundreds of pounds, even thousands, for what might seem routine tasks.

Bodily, the same applies. Because of the Countach's impossible vision from most angles and heavy controls, it's quite possible that parking damage might have been sustained on the very vulnerable extremities of the car. The all-aluminium bodywork (with the exception of the wheel arch extensions on 'S' models) is, naturally, very expensive to repair and even though replacement panels are available they are extremely expensive and likely not to fit as well as the original as each car is virtually tailor-made around its constituent parts. Some idea of repair costs can be gauged by the price of some of the components: £852 for a front wing, £74.50 for a front light unit. £901.39 for a windscreen ...

When contemplating purchase of a Countach, consider for a moment the service costs: a set of front brake pads cost £195.50, tyres range from £230.35 (front) to £334.02 (rear) each. A complete exhaust system is £602.90. And remember that service intervals are 5000 miles for an oil change and minor check-over to a full service at 10,000 mile intervals.

Of course, if you are fortunate enough to be able to contemplate the purchase of a Countach, then none of this should be a problem – the Countach is a car of very high performance and, as with all the best things, it has to be paid for.

That aside, a well maintained and properly serviced Countach should provide many hours of trouble free and exhilarating motoring and, providing care and attention is paid at the buying stage, the car need not present any more problems than those associated with much lesser machinery.

As always with cars of this type, buying from an experienced dealer such as Portman Lamborghini or Barry Martina's Fulham-based Heathman's garage will probably be the safest bet. Cars on offer from either outlet are more likely to have been properly serviced and looked after by trained personnel than those offered privately or through non-specialist dealers. In any event always scrutinize the car's service history prior to purchase.

CLUBS, SPECIALISTS & BOOKS

Clubs & Specialists

In Britain, membership of the *Lamborghini Owners Club* is almost a necessity for owners of the marque. Run enthusiastically by Lamborghini specialist, Barry Martina, the attractions include social gatherings throughout the country and organised test days at leading race circuits. Quite often these events are run in association with other clubs catering for similar cars, for example the De Tomaso Owners Club and the Ferrari Owners Club, and they allow owners to exploit their cars' full performance potential in controlled conditions – very popular when today's speed limit-ridden roads are considered!

The Lamborghini Owners Club is truly international with many members coming from overseas to take part in activities organised by the British contingent. The glossy magazine is produced quarterly which keeps members in touch with all that is going on.

Barry Martina runs Heathman's garage, in Heathman's Yard, Fulham, London SW6, telephone 01-731 1962.

Portman Lamborghini of London have for many years handled the UK import and distribution of all Lamborghini cars

and must be regarded as the experts on all aspects of the marque. Whether you are interested in buying new or second-hand or getting the first-rate service the marque demands, Portman are the first people to contact. The full address is:

Portman Lamborghini Ltd,
108 George Street,
London W1H 5RL

Finally, Barry Robinson, whose beautiful red Countach LP500S I was so privileged to borrow both for photography and driving purposes, should be mentioned as he runs a business specialising in the hire, with or without fully experienced drivers, of the Countach.

A new Countach Quattrovalvole joined his fleet in the spring of 1986 and enquiries on the hiring of this car or the LP500S should be directed to: **Lamborghini Hire,** 108 George Street, London W1, telephone 01-459 3000.

Books

Literature on the Lamborghini Countach is limited. Probably the most authoritative history is the Osprey **Autohistory** by Peter Coltrin and Jean-François

Marchet, a hardback book of some 135 pages covering the conception, development and history of the car from the very beginning. Plenty of black and white pictures add to the text, though there have been developments, including the introduction of the *Quattrovalvole*, since the book was written. Recently the book was revised and updated.

Providing a complete history of the Lamborghini marque is the massive work by Jean-Marc Borel, entitled simply **Lamborghini.** It is written in three languages, Italian, English and French. Every car made by Lamborghini is depicted in full colour together with a short 'potted' history and a comprehensive specification table. The story is told in reasonable detail, though perhaps something is lost in the translation.

Another useful addition to the Countach library is the Brooklands Books compilation of road tests carried out by magazines of the motoring press around the world. Included are tests from *Motor, Autosport, Thoroughbred and Classic Cars, Road and Track, Autocar* and *Car* together with others from Australia and America. The cut-off date, however, is 1982 so the *Quattrovalvole* is not covered.

With this Haynes *Super Profile,* I have tried to give a basic background to the development of the Countach with reference to the fascinating history of the Lamborghini company itself. With that in mind, hopefully the continuing story will provide material for further books for many years to come.

PHOTO GALLERY

1. Ferruccio Lamborghini with his V12 back in 1963. The reflection of his first car, the 350 GTV, is just visible in the mirrors behind. At this time the engine was fitted with a ZF gearbox. Twin distributors and six down-draught carburettors feature. (Autocar/QPL)

2. The first Lamborghini ever made, the 350GTV, produced in 1963. Franco Scaglione's body styling was criticised heavily at the time but not the magnificent V12 engine, a development of which today powers the Countach. (Autocar/QPL)

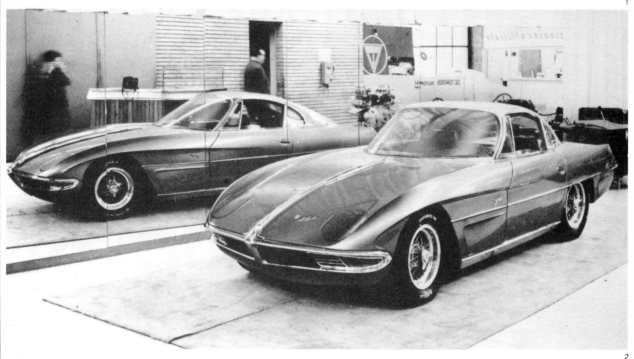

3. The first Miura on display at the Turin Motor Show in 1966, surely one of the most beautiful GTs ever made. This photo was taken on the Bertone stand. (Autocar/QPL)

4. This is how the Countach LP500 looked when it first appeared at the Geneva Show in 1971. The purity of line was not cluttered by the air scoop 'ears' and NACA ducts. Some features of this car were not carried over to later production versions, including the periscope rear view mirror and external door handles. This is the original prototype, completed just in time for the show and driven over the Alps from Italy by Bob Wallace. Once again it is displayed on the Bertone stand. (Autocar/QPL)

5. The Countach LP400 as it appeared at the Geneva Motor Show in 1973. Even though this was the official début of the car as a production model, it was not to be for sale for another two years. Note twin windscreen wipers. (Autocar/QPL)

6. Another view of that same car. Since 1973 NACA ducts and air scoop 'ears' had been added to assist engine cooling. (Autocar/QPL)

7. An early Countach bodyshell taking shape in the Lamborghini factory in the early Seventies. The cockpit incorporates a neat roll cage in its construction. (Autocar/QPL)

8. Countach LP500S: the car in its latest development guise. The rear wing, fitted to this car, reduces the top speed owing to its extra drag but is essential for stability.

7

8

9 & 10. Rear view shows the enormous size of the tyres and rear wing. Glassfibre wheel arch extensions are essential to cover the tyres.

9

10

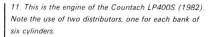

11

11. This is the engine of the Countach LP400S (1982). Note the use of two distributors, one for each bank of six cylinders.

12. The engine of Barry Robinson's LP500S is fully blueprinted and balanced and develops marginally more brake horsepower than the standard item. The 'Quattrovalvole' engine, introduced in 1985 features Weber 44DCNF downdraught carburettors, centrally-mounted over the engine.

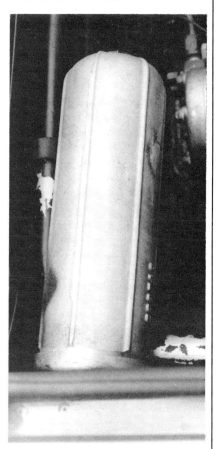

12

13

13. The oil filter housing, together with certain other parts of the Countach engine, are extremely expensive magnesium Elektron castings.

14. Sump casting for the Countach engine on the jig in the factory. From this shot it is easy to see how the unique driveshaft-under-crankshaft system works. The crankcase fits on top of this once the driveshaft is in position, a simple and effective way of overcoming the problems of mounting the engine longitudinally in a mid-engined car. Note also the differential housing cast integrally with the sump. (Autocar/QPL)

14

15

16

15. The engine cover lifts right up to give reasonable access to the engine. Most major service items are readily accessible on the Countach.

16. The modest size of the rear boot allows space for a couple of suitcases and no more. Well this is a driving machine after all ...

17. Barry Robinson's LP500S with its doors and hatches open. The operation of the doors is very satisfactory giving plenty of open space for access to the cockpit.

17

18

18. Four powerful quartz halogen headlamps are housed in aerodynamic harmony ...

19. ... until raised electronically into the pop-up position!

20. The indicator/sidelight covers are electronically heated.

21. Carello Spotlamps are fitted as standard each side of the number plate.

22. Detail of the moulded front spoiler which blends into the frontal aspect of the Countach S.

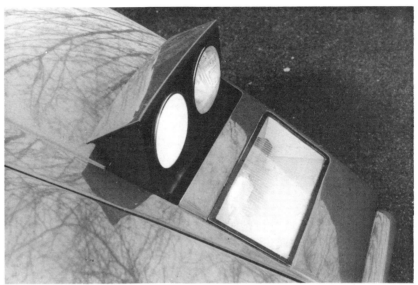

19

20

21

22

23. These mirrors were fitted to earlier models of the Countach S, LP400 and don't appear to fit very well with the car's image ...

24. ... Compare the LP400 mirrors with these on the LP500S.

25. Louvres in the rear wings expel air from the radiators – and provide dramatic effect! That rear aerofoil is essential to keep the back down at high speed.

26. The rear lights are set into a panel of reflective Perspex.

27. The view most drivers are likely to have of the Countach. Purposeful and mean, this is surely the most aggressive view of the car.

23

24

25

26

27

28. A single pantograph action wiper covers the whole of the vast screen which is actually slightly curved despite its impression of being flat.

28

29

29. Cooling air is ducted to the radiators through these louvres, assisted by the ears. The latter were fitted to the Countach after the prototype experienced cooling problems.

30. These NACA ducts help to channel cooling air to the radiators situated below the louvres above. Note the door button on the top face. From this shot the quality of the panel fit is evident with a perfectly straight line between door and shell; remarkable for doors that open upwards.

31. The door shut conceals the remote controls for the boot and rear engine cover. The door latch is likely to cause greasy marks on one's clothes when entering and leaving the car.

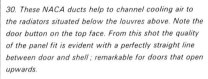

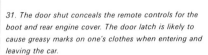

30

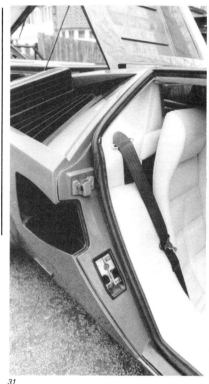

31

32. The author demonstrating the astounding lowness of the car, and the preferred method of entry.

32

33. This shot shows the driving position for a right-hand drive car. Note left-hand handbrake, and boot on steering column for rake and fore/aft adjustment. It is just possible to see the rake of the windscreen pillar (centre top) from this angle.

34. This car is fitted with a remote control Blaupunkt stereo radio/ cassette with the control handily situated near the driver. This fitment is essential as it is virtually impossible to reach the facia from the driving position with the seatbelt on!

35. Driver's eye view of the Countach. Large expanses of hand-stitched leather and the vast central console dominate the cabin. Instruments are prone to reflections. Three air vents provide demisting for the vast screen but are not too effective.

33

34

35

36

37

38

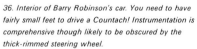

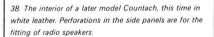

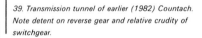

36. Interior of Barry Robinson's car. You need to have fairly small feet to drive a Countach! Instrumentation is comprehensive though likely to be obscured by the thick-rimmed steering wheel.

37. The only difference between the interior of this 1983 and earlier models is the addition of extra padding on the centre console ahead of the gearlever, plus the relocation of some minor switchgear.

38. The interior of a later model Countach, this time in white leather. Perforations in the side panels are for the fitting of radio speakers.

39. Transmission tunnel of earlier (1982) Countach. Note detent on reverse gear and relative crudity of switchgear.

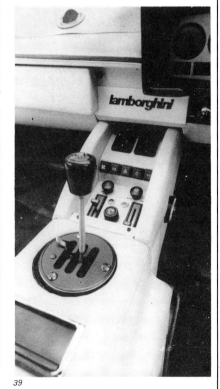

39

41

42

40. Vestigial and practically useless rear screen. On the latest models the view is further obscured by raised portion of engine cover over the now centrally-located carburettors.

41. Spartan door trim treatment. Note the tiny opening of 'window,' manual operation and doorbin. The door opening handle is situated at the top of the bin, out of sight in this shot.

42. The simple design of the later production window winder handle. As the maximum opening is only a few inches, its construction does not have to be very substantial!

43. 'Spacesaver' tyre fits in the front boot together with battery and master cylinder.

44. The master cylinder is situated under the front bonnet. The clutch cylinder is just visible below it to the right.

43

44

45

46

45. The famous 'Raging Bull' emblem, the hallmark of the Lamborghini name. Under the Mimran ownership, the bull emblem was reversed for a while but eventually returned to its original state.

46. Close up of the 'telephone dial' Countach wheels – made by Campagnolo – and their thin band of Pirelli P7 rubber tucked away neatly under those wide wheel arches.

47. Simple script on the rear panel denotes engine size. 'S' figure harks back to old Miura days.

48. The 'Quattrovavole' engine, introduced in 1985, showing the new central position of the down-draught carburettors.

47

48

49

50

49. The prototype Countach LP500 awaiting its final test run into the concrete block at MIRA to satisfy the E-marking requirements for the production Countach. Several features of this car were not carried over to subsequent production versions, including the 'periscope' rear view mirror. (Autocar/QPL)

50. Pop rivets around the louvres and air intake 'ears' shows this to be the prototype. A host of electronic measuring equipment was fitted to the car when it was crash tested. (Autocar/QPL)

51. After impact. Notice how little distortion is evident in the overall structure of the car. The door has moved but has not burst open in the crash. (Autocar/QPL)

52. This shot shows how little damage was sustained within the cockpit. Although the steering column has moved back the cabin is basically intact. (Autocar/QPL)

51

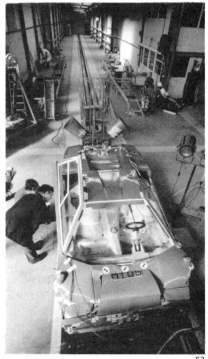

52

53

53. Though flattened at the front, the door still opens normally. Even the windscreen is still in one piece. (Autocar/QPL)

54. & 55. These two shots show the level of distortion experienced by the steering wheel in the Countach after impacting into the concrete block. Top, before impact, note the angle of the steering wheel. Bottom, after impact, the wheel has moved up and the door has distorted along its bottom shut face but the overall shape of the cockpit has not altered drastically, proof of the Countach's immense overall strength. (Autocar/QPL)

54

55

56

56. The Lamborghini factory in Sant'Agata Bolognese
photographed in 1985.